Cambridge Elements

Elements in Historical Theory and Practice
edited by
Daniel Woolf
Queen's University, Ontario

CONTESTED PUBLIC MONUMENTS

Global Perspectives on Landscapes of Memory

Maria Grever
Erasmus University Rotterdam and NL-Lab, KNAW Humanities Cluster

Shaftesbury Road, Cambridge CB2 8EA, United Kingdom

One Liberty Plaza, 20th Floor, New York, NY 10006, USA

477 Williamstown Road, Port Melbourne, VIC 3207, Australia

314–321, 3rd Floor, Plot 3, Splendor Forum, Jasola District Centre, New Delhi – 110025, India

103 Penang Road, #05–06/07, Visioncrest Commercial, Singapore 238467

Cambridge University Press is part of Cambridge University Press & Assessment, a department of the University of Cambridge.

We share the University's mission to contribute to society through the pursuit of education, learning and research at the highest international levels of excellence.

www.cambridge.org
Information on this title: www.cambridge.org/9781009515689

DOI: 10.1017/9781009515702

© Maria Grever 2025

This publication is in copyright. Subject to statutory exception and to the provisions of relevant collective licensing agreements, no reproduction of any part may take place without the written permission of Cambridge University Press & Assessment.

When citing this work, please include a reference to the DOI 10.1017/9781009515702

First published 2025

A catalogue record for this publication is available from the British Library

ISBN 978-1-009-51568-9 Hardback
ISBN 978-1-009-51571-9 Paperback
ISSN 2634-8616 (online)
ISSN 2634-8608 (print)

Cambridge University Press & Assessment has no responsibility for the persistence or accuracy of URLs for external or third-party internet websites referred to in this publication and does not guarantee that any content on such websites is, or will remain, accurate or appropriate.

For EU product safety concerns, contact us at Calle de José Abascal, 56, 1°, 28003 Madrid, Spain, or email eugpsr@cambridge.org

Contested Public Monuments

Global Perspectives on Landscapes of Memory

Elements in Historical Theory and Practice

DOI: 10.1017/9781009515702
First published online: October 2025

Maria Grever
Erasmus University Rotterdam and NL-Lab, KNAW Humanities Cluster
Author for correspondence: Maria Grever, grever@eshcc.eur.nl

Abstract: In the new millennium, many public monuments around the world have become the target of protests as part of social movements' struggles against inequality and discrimination. Despite research into the significance of toppled statues or damaged monuments and the motives of activists, little attention has been paid to the extent to which iconoclastic activism changes the narratives of public spaces or landscapes of memory. This Element approaches current conflicts over public monuments as an attempt to transform the mnemonic regime of public spaces. It examines global cases involving colonialism, Black slavery, world wars, and women's oppression. Using theoretical concepts, such as monumental narrativity, necropolitical space, white innocence, and the implicated subject, four current contexts of contestations will be highlighted: the fabric of landscapes of memory; the relationship between the living and the dead of a community; the power of visual language, iconography, and multiplication; the importance of dialogical monuments.

Keywords: contested public monuments, landscapes of memory, monumental narrativity, colonialism, gender

© Maria Grever 2025

ISBNs: 9781009515689 (HB), 9781009515719 (PB), 9781009515702 (OC)
ISSNs: 2634-8616 (online), 2634-8608 (print)

Contents

1 Introduction — 1

2 Landscapes of Memory and Monumental Narrativity — 6

3 Monuments and Necropolitical Space — 18

4 Iconography, Visual Language, and Multiplication — 36

5 Dialogical Monuments in a Global Media Network — 53

6 Conclusion — 72

Bibliography — 76

1 Introduction

Today it is difficult to imagine that American politicians in the early nineteenth century were reluctant to erect monumental memorials to their leaders. 'True memory lay not in a heap of dead stones but in the hearts and the minds of the people; no monument could substitute for living social memory, nourished by liberty and education', they argued.[1] The aversion to monuments came from several sources, such as the Republican critique of the English monarchy and the Puritan hostility toward public images. About fifty years later this view had completely changed. Impressive monuments and statues had spread all over the country and not only in the United States. The emergence and development of nation-states in Europe and other Western countries incited the making of heroic tangible representations in cities and villages. In Germany and France, for example, civic monument movements were organized to raise money for the erection of gigantic statues in honour of the now nationalized historical figures Hermann (Arminius) and Vercingetorix from Roman times.[2] A stimulating factor was that from the last quarter of the nineteenth century, the production of public monuments and statues was no longer as expensive as it used to be. Production increasingly became a commercial affair. Initiated by leading politicians and enthusiastically supported by large groups of citizens, statues that radiated national pride were erected well into the twentieth century. As political powers changed, so did the controversies over statues and monuments.

The aforementioned early American aversion to monuments is one of the few exceptions in history, because since ancient times countless monuments have been created in public spaces – whether in the form of stone circles, pyramids, monumental columns, or equestrian statues – as materialized reminders of historical events, military leaders, monarchs, and gods for future generations. The erection of these material constructions seems like an attempt to overcome the ravages of time and oblivion to which even the greatest kings and leaders are subject. But ever since their inception in human history, monuments can turn into hated objects that underlie the escalation of hostilities during socio-political uprisings, riots, and protests.[3] Defacing, inscribing, tearing down, or destroying statues usually express anger and resistance against a particular regime and its leaders. Some scholars call these practices a form of 'de-commemoration', emphasizing the continuity of (re)transforming material representations in public space.[4] Public monuments and statues can also serve as important places of mourning, as signs of solidarity, pride, and identity for a particular community or as daily anchor points for people's temporal-spatial orientation.

---

[1] Savage 2009, 1.   [2] Tacke 1995, 23.   [3] Freedberg 2016, 68.
[4] Gensburger and Wüstenberg 2023, 3–4.

The current conflicts over public monuments demonstrate a need to change the landscape of memory in cities and other areas. An important background to this phenomenon is the growing resistance of ethnic (migrant) groups and other cultural communities against historical figures on a pedestal that perpetuate their discrimination and lack of recognition in society.[5] Activists consider these historic representations in public spaces as symbolic violence against the victims of colonial exploitation, enslavement, and racism. Social movements such as Black Lives Matter have gained significant international attention in their opposition to discriminatory monuments. Protests intensified in 2020 after the killing of unarmed black American man George Floyd by two police officers in Minneapolis (see Figure 1).

Emotions can also run high at public monuments that were erected after a major war. For example, when it turns out that certain groups of victims have been ignored or when perpetrators' heritage is restored. But often people walk

Figure 1 Defaced statue of Confederate general J.E.B. Stuart during protests following the murder of George Floyd. Richmond (USA) 2020. Photo Tyler Walter. https://commons.wikimedia.org/wiki/File: JEB_Stuart_Monument_2020-05-31.jpg

---

[5] Demetriou and Wingo 2018.

past a monument without thinking. Many material constructions are like street furniture, wedged between traffic.[6] At most, they function as a meeting place for people from their neighbourhood, regardless of its representation. It is also possible that public monuments have not caused any commotion for decades, only to suddenly become the object of collective protest. Something has probably been smouldering for a while without being noticed. Seemingly out of nowhere, monuments and statues are defaced or covered with cloth. Most of these activists are seeking recognition of (formerly) oppressed communities and their legacy of injustice and inequality in the present.[7] In response, counter-demonstrators sometimes protect the monuments. Its tangibility mobilizes supporters and opponents. Despite the online possibilities to visualize the past with 'fleeting images on screen', the appeal of monuments in public space has apparently not disappeared.[8]

Central to this Element are (semi-)permanent monuments of historical figures and events in public spaces that are contested today. The term contested points to the different interpretations of the ideological meaning of public monuments, expressed in debates or demonstrations. Vandalism – damaging or defacing without a purpose, just 'for fun', often in a drunken mood – is not part of it.[9]

Much research has been done into the motives, causes and circumstances under which monuments, memorials, statues, obelisks, and other material representations have become the target of protests and iconoclasm.[10] Important factors include the location of a monument, its size, posture, and its interaction with the public and the media. Protests against statues can also arise because deceased leaders resisted having their likeness set in stone. For example, Sioux leader Crazy Horse in South Dakota never wanted to be photographed or filmed. Today, people of the Sioux Nation oppose to the construction of the Crazy Horse Memorial in the Black Hills, 26 km. southwest of Mount Rushmore National Memorial, which features the four American presidents. They argue 'that a man so contrary to having his image captured on film would never agree to have it sprawled across the face of a mountain, and his undisclosed burial site would seem to indicate the same.'[11] Scholars have also investigated what happens after the toppling of a statue, its so-called afterlife, and the extent to which activists have been successful in calling for a monument to be removed or a new memorial to be erected in recognition of a community.[12] The findings show that contested public monuments play a major role in social movements' struggles against

---

[6] Shanken, 2022. [7] Grever 2023; Rigney 2023. [8] Huyssen 1994, 12. [9] Réau 1959.
[10] E.g. Balkenhol 2020; Branscome 2021; Kapp 2021; Gensburger and Wüstenberg 2023.
[11] See https://honormonument.org/2023/12/24/the-crazy-horse-memorial-colossal-and-controversial/.
[12] E.g. Larsen 2012; Rigney 2018; Çelik 2020.

inequality and discrimination in society. Recent protests against colonial statues are not so much aiming at a political regime change, Ann Rigney argues, but about 'a change in the collective narrative, and, indirectly, of social relations in the present.'[13] Another related, but less explored, issue is the extent to which iconoclastic activism leads to mnemonic change in public spaces, termed as 'landscapes of memory'.

This Element approaches *current conflicts over public monuments as an attempt to change the mnemonic regime expressed in landscapes of memory.* The aim is not to provide a comprehensive overview, since the phenomenon is too broad for that. Instead, the monuments studied mainly concern historical processes and traumatic events that have a long-term impact on the lives of large groups of people. Therefore, three overlapping research areas are addressed: colonialism, slavery, and apartheid; world wars and genocides; women's oppression and sexual exploitation. The contestations will be illustrated by a range of trans-national and global cases from the Americas, Asia, Europe, and South-Africa.

The terms monument and memorial overlap in meaning and are often used interchangeably in research and public debate. In general, a monument means a three-dimensional sculpture or built structure that often, but not always, commemorates an event or person in a venerable and respectful manner, while memorial is more associated with loss, leaning toward mourning and grief.[14] For the sake of readability, in this Element the term monument will be used for any public physical representation. Where necessary, the specific form is indicated such as bust, triumphal arch, obelisk, gravestone, plaque, site of remembrance. Names of streets, bridges, tunnels, schools, and other buildings are not included or only mentioned in passing.

The erection, unveiling, and restoration of public monuments and memorials imply the recognition that they provide an officially sanctioned view of history. Every public representation is a performative statement: a non-verbal message that a particular person, group, or event deserves exclusive attention in the public space. Consequently and paradoxically, they also encourage oblivion, especially when a statue honours someone whose history is complex and layered.[15] Interpretations of the past resonate through public monuments, which in turn evoke new histories and can have a substantive influence on education, museums, and (social) media. Moving the monument to another location or altering the design can compromise its expressiveness, undermining the intentions of commissioners and artists to capture a specific ideology or message. Pulling down monuments that refer to a divided past can evoke strong emotions.

---

[13] Rigney 2022, 10.   [14] Wagoner and Bresco 2022.
[15] Gensburger and Wüstenberg 2023, 3–4.

To better understand the conflicts over monuments worldwide, I use insights from memory studies, narrative philosophy, anthropology, and genocide studies. Four contexts of contestations will be highlighted: the (one-sided) fabric of a landscape of memory; the need for a monument to prevent amnesia and to restore the relationship with ancestors; the power of monuments through visual language, iconography and multiplication; and the effects of deliberate monumental interventions and disruptive monuments on the public. Some theoretical concepts will provide further insights into the meaning and background of public monumental conflicts and the attempts at mnemonic change.

In the following Section 2, the overarching concept *landscapes of memory* is introduced. Its meaning refers to a mediated externalized cultural archive in the public space that can have a major impact on the well-being of different communities in a country. Brief but explicit attention is also paid to the rather hybrid concept of public space. The conflicts about the many Columbus monuments in Argentina and the US clarify how plural and dynamic public space actually is. Drawing on Paul Ricoeur's theory of narrative philosophy, I will then explain how landscapes of memory are condensed time-spaces that change over time. This theory, translated as *monumental narrativity*, makes it more understandable how and why individuals and groups of people can experience a public memory landscape as exclusive and one-sided, but also how these narratives can change and be (re)appropriated by city dwellers and passers-by.

Section 3 explores how tangible memorials support the *necropolitical space*, a concept developed by Hans Ruin that relates to the space in which the living and the dead are brought together in a mutual relationship across generations. Public funerals and monuments express this relationship. But interaction with the dead can change over time or be disrupted due to large-scale violence against a community. This latter process is clarified with striking historical cases. One of these is the contested statue of the colonial Governor-General J.P. Coen in the Netherlands. The statue's current location and proud stance seem to conceal the massacre that took place under Coen's responsibility in 1621. The controversy demonstrates a form of *colonial aphasia*, a concept developed by Ann Stoler.

Section 4 focuses on iconography, visual language, and multiplication. A first case is the *hegemonic presence* of monuments to Queen Victoria around the world to confirm British rule over the empire and the subsequent anti-colonial iconoclastic protests. Another case is statues of missionaries with (half-)naked black indigenous children. Using the concept of *white innocence*, coined by Gloria Wekker, its condescending and racist imagery is scrutinized. The importance of location and relocation of a monument within a memory landscape is then discussed. The cases include the exact placement of stumbling stones in European countries in memory of Holocaust victims, and the conflicts over the (re)location of the so-called Bronze Soldier monument of 'Soviet liberators' in Estonia. This section also reflects on the limits of representing the unspeakable atrocities of war and genocide. Gradually, from the late 1970s onwards, the emphasis shifted from mimetic statues of national heroes to aniconic monuments, such as abstract sculptures and walls of names.

Section 5 discusses the dialogical potential of monuments in a multi-dynamic global media network. The emphasis here is on interactive public interventions, such as anti-monuments, compensation monuments and counter-monuments in Colombia, South-Africa, and Germany. Despite these artistic experiments and the call for decolonizing memory landscapes, public representations of women remain rare. A notable exception are statues of 'comfort women', a euphemism for female sex slaves used by the Japanese during the Second World War. The impact of such disruptive monuments is discussed further in light of Hannah Arendt's ideas on 'Action' in the public sphere as *modes of action*. In line with her philosophy of lived experience, I will show that certain innovative monuments can be conceived as public interventions that trigger (self)reflection, plurality and dialogue, while at the same time clarifying – in terms of Michael Rothberg – the *implicated subject* position.

The conclusion in Section 6 presents a synthesizing view on the meanings of contested public monuments as embedded in a memory landscape and as part of a dynamic and global media network.

2 Landscapes of Memory and Monumental Narrativity

Today, many parks, squares, and streets feature city- and state-sanctioned public monuments and memorials that celebrate past victories or commemorate the victims who died in battles and wars. They affirm and enhance the self-respect and well-being of dominant communities, while the existence of less powerful groups is usually ignored.[16] In this sense, public monuments are a value-related selection of collective memories. Whereas a cultural or mental archive is metaphorically located in the hearts and minds of people with ingrained images and prejudices about colonialism and racism,[17] public monuments are the externalized materialized representations of this archive, including views on citizenship and nationhood. They are products of socio-cultural and political differences between communities, based as much on processes of canonization as on (unintentional) amnesia. Conversely, their tangibility can evoke forgotten memories and old stories, which are activated when monuments are seen and touched.

---

[16] Solnit 2017.   [17] Said 1994, xxiii–xxiv; Wekker 2016, 2.

Landscapes of Memory and Public Space

Conflicts over monuments can only be properly understood if the environment or landscape in which they are embedded is also taken into account. Contemporary research on this subject is quite diverse and multidisciplinary. In his edited volume *The Place of Landscape*, philosopher Jeff Malpas draws attention to the conception of landscape as a representational construction, presented as an object and seen from a certain view, which always implies separation and detachment.[18] In the same volume, Phillip Sheldrake considers landscape an ambiguous concept. Following Simon Schama's *Landscape and Memory*, he argues that landscapes provide the physical features upon which human beings can project their imaginations to shape distinctive identities and to express ideologies. Sheldrake also emphasizes that landscapes, whether real or imagined, are always linked to power differences.[19]

Archaeologists and geographers have elaborated a landscape-biographical approach: the history or biography of a landscape. Their starting-point is that landscapes are no passive by-products of anonymous economic and social developments, but connected to the life-histories and social environment of individuals and communities.[20] Sociologists, anthropologists, and experts in memory studies focus on landscape traces of a war, social conflict, or another catastrophe with concepts such as 'commemorative landscape', 'memorial landscape', or 'memory-scape'.[21] Monuments, statues, and other physical representations can be considered as part of a mnemonic regime that guides people to orient themselves in place and time. When people walk or cycle in a neighbourhood or city, existing buildings, monuments, statues, and street names function as spatial and temporal landmarks that authorize specific dominant and selective memories of the past. In this way, the landscape functions as a mnemonic device: a system that helps people remember, that confirms, perpetuates, and develops cultural memories. At the same time, it contributes to the transmission of collective values, ideologies, and narratives, possibly including the histories of families and distant ancestors. Such a landscape or environment can become a major building block of identity and memory.[22]

In most of these studies, public space and place are dynamic and activity-oriented phenomena. In this context Gunnar Maus proposes the concept 'landscape of memory' in order to pay attention to place-based memory-making, understood as a social phenomenon of localized memory. Although he assesses

---

[18] Malpas ed. 2011, 6.   [19] Schama 1995; Sheldrake 2011, 183.
[20] Samuels 1979; Kolen, Renes and Hermans eds. 2015.
[21] Van der Schriek 2019; Simko, Cunningham and Fox 2022; Rofe and Ripmeester 2023.
[22] Gropas 2007, 531; Lindström 2008, 227.

each term as ambiguous, the combination clarifies what Maus calls 'practices of localized memory' that contextualize their 'human carriers (...) and the physical world they engage with as material arrangements'.[23]

The concept landscape of memory in this Element implies an extensive, more or less demarcated public space as a mnemonic device with symbolic, historical, and material (physical) meanings through which people can move in different ways. More specifically, the term landscape refers to the public space of a socio-political geographical entity, for example a city, province, nation, or trans-national region. The term memory denotes to what Jan Assmann has called cultural memory: the construction and transmission of (shared or imposed) memories of a community that are written down, archived or visualized in rituals, durable photos, sculptures, and monuments.[24] A landscape of memory therefore contains symbolic meanings and materialized representations of events, persons, and communities from the past, often situated in (historically) characteristic public places and initiated by the political elite or a collective that has acquired some power. The concept combines at least four basic, interrelated dimensions: time, space, representation (including aesthetics), and human practices (including action and emotion).[25] Each landscape has its own biography with different historical layers and a spatial layout of monuments, statues, and memorials.[26] Local, regional, and (trans)national landscapes of memory can overlap and change over time.

Some sociologists and anthropologists also examine the landscape traces of a specific war, social conflict or other catastrophe. In these studies a memory landscape is not only a stage where rituals and other commemorative actions take place; the landscape also stages action, it is itself part of the actual performance.[27] A striking example of a memory landscape of a specific war is the region around Ypres in Belgium in the Flemish Westhoek, where a long and terrible battle took place in the First World War. Large and small cemeteries are scattered throughout this region. The Allied war graves have rows of spotless gravestones, often surrounded by walls and an impressive entrance; the Germans have inconspicuous cemeteries that are located in the back. There are remains of British bunkers in the hills, and old and restored trenches.[28] The major commemoration of eighty years of D-Day on 6 June, 2024 in Normandy also took place on and around the original invasion beaches.

A memory landscape is a specific kind of public space. This concept comes close to what philosophers, notably Jürgen Habermas, call the public sphere

---

[23] Maus 2015, 217. [24] Assmann 2008. [25] Grever 2024, 153.
[26] Van der Schriek 2019, 100. [27] Samuels 1979; Johnson 2005. [28] Eskes 2023.

(*Öffentlichkeit*): a domain where ideas and information can be exchanged informally on matters of interest to the public – often, but not always – with opposing or diverging views expressed by participants in a discussion. From the late eighteenth century onwards, these public gatherings and debates of citizens gradually resulted in what Habermas considers a 'civil society': a space of free interaction between autonomous subjects.[29] According to critical theorist Nancy Fraser, the public sphere in Habermas' sense can be seen as 'a theatre in modern societies in which political participation is enacted through the medium of talk. It is the space in which citizens deliberate about common affairs (...).'[30] In this arena, which is conceptually distinct from the state and the private sphere, public opinion is formed. Yet not everyone had the same access to this, Fraser argues. Since the 1780s, the public sphere emerged as a bourgeois *male public space*, the training ground and power base of bourgeois men who were coming to see themselves as a universal class, 'preparing to assert their fitness to govern.'[31] This public sphere dominated at the expense of alternative publics (e.g., women, labourers, colonized people), preventing them from articulating their concerns.

There is still no equal access to the public sphere. What is considered general and important depends on hegemonic discourses, often resulting in the formation of other less visible public spaces with different publics (see also Section 5). Hence, the public sphere or public space is no monolithic entity but consists of a hierarchical variety of publics and counter-publics operating with different (overlapping) interpretative frameworks, different criteria for participation and styles of communication.[32] Recently, scholars have also reflected on public activism from a gender perspective that strive for more inclusive public spaces, such as streets, parks, university campuses, examining the infrastructures that make up public space.[33] Supporters and opponents of specific monuments illustrate the dynamics between publics and counter-publics and the ways in which they – often alongside each other – make their voices heard in their attempts to change the public landscapes of memory.

Columbus Monuments in the Americas

The conflicts over monuments erected to Christopher Columbus in the Americas are revealing in this regard. Opponents who advocate for the destruction – often indigenous communities – view Columbus' arrival as the start of forced conversions to Christianity, racism and ultimately the extermination of millions of local

---

[29] Habermas 1989.   [30] Fraser 1990, 57.
[31] Fraser 1990, 60; Grever and Waaldijk 2004, 14–16.   [32] Weisser 2008.
[33] Gquola et al. 2024, 1.

people, including their ancestors. Supporters – often descendants of formerly discriminated Italian immigrants who are proud of this 'discoverer of the new world' – organize counter-protests with the aim to protect the monuments. A telling case is what happened in Argentina.

In 2013, Argentine president Cristina Fernández de Kirchner decided to replace the large Columbus monument opposite the presidential palace Casa Rosada in Buenos Aires' Plazo Mayo (central square) with a statue of nineteenth-century guerilla leader Juana Azurduy de Padilla.[34] Azurduy, who had indigenous roots, was horrified by the enslavement of the indigenous people in Spain's silver mines and became a passionate ally of the indigenous revolutionary movement. She married fellow revolutionary Manuel Ascencio Padilla, with whom she had five children. Together they fought for Bolivian and Argentine independence. After the capture and murder of her husband by the Spanish, she continued the fight and won several victories. Nevertheless, at her death in 1862, Juana was almost forgotten. She was not commemorated until a century later (see Figure 2).

Kirchner considered Azurduy a heroine of independence, someone who represented the forgotten and suppressed history of the nation's indigenous

Figure 2 Anonymous portrait of military leader Juana Azurduy, ca. 1857. https://en.wikipedia.org/wiki/Juana_Azurduy_de_Padilla#/media/File: Juana_Azurduy.jpg

---

[34] Frei 2019. See for the relocation of the Juana Azurduy Monument to the Kirchner Cultural Centre, YouTube: https://wanderwomenproject.com/places/juana-azurduy-monument/.

populations, and of women in particular. To honour her, she commissioned a bronze statue of the guerrilla leader, co-financed by the Bolivian president Evo Morales. The statue was to replace the Columbus monument near the Plaza de Mayo. However, led by mayor Mauritio Macri of Buenos Aires, local Italian associations, and other organizations strongly protested against its relocation and organized counter-removal demonstrations. Lawsuits followed. The monument had become a political flashpoint between the president's center-left government and the conservative Buenos Aires mayor of Italian descent.[35]

Despite all protests, Kirchner persevered and engaged Argentine artist and indigenous rights activist Andrés Zerneri. In three years he constructed with a team of assistants an immense monument of 15,8 metre. Meanwhile, while legal processes were still ongoing, dismantling of the base of the Columbus monument began. For two years its marble pieces lay on the ground. The Argentine Italian community was outraged. Then the president and Macri finally reached a compromise. The Columbus monument would be rebuilt elsewhere in the city on the coast near the airport. After a public hearing the city's legislature and the National Parliament voted in favour of the relocation. The idea for the accord came from *Identidad Territorial Malalweche*, an organization representing hundred indigenous communities. For them, the marble memory of Columbus did not have to disappear completely. They particularly objected to the symbolism of its prominent location within the urban memory landscape of Buenos Aires (see also Section 4).[36]

In 2015, the larger-than-life bronze statue of Juana Azurduy was unveiled. Aesthetically, the impressive statue seemed quite traditional as it literally depicts a tough, combative guerrilla fighter. But the difference was that this time for once a female leader stood on a pedestal.

Due to hasty construction using metals that showed oxidation, the statue began to fall apart after only five months. Macri, who had succeeded Kirchner as the new Argentine president, had the monument examined. The conclusion was that it had to be removed for repairs. After artist Zerneri had restored the monument, in 2017, it was moved to the Plaza del Correo, in front of the Kirchner Cultural Centre, where it still stands (see photos and video about the relocation of the monument https://wanderwomenproject.com/places/juana-azurduy-monument/).

Looking back, it is striking how little consultation had taken place with indigenous people, even though the whole issue concerned their own history. During the disputes over the replacement of the Columbus monument, members

---

[35] Ryback, Ellis and Glahn eds. 2021, 230–232.
[36] Ryback, Ellis and Glahn eds. 2021, 234–235.

of the Qom indigenous community held a vigil at the Plazo de Mayo. They demanded 'an audience with Kirchner, advocating that hostilities towards their people be stopped.' Later, the Mapuche Confederation of the indigenous Neuquén people also criticized the erection of the Azurduy statue. In a statement they denounced the initiative as one of the 'numerous symbolic and rhetorical acts, loaded with demagoguery and resignation', which indigenous communities were expected to 'uncritically applaud [. . .] while dispossession and expulsion of communitarian territories continues'.[37] According to historian Cheryl Frei the 'monuments – one representing Argentina's previously maligned Italian immigrant heritage, the other its forgotten indigenous culture – demonstrate how the fundamental struggle for national identity has been embedded and contested in the capital's urban landscape in ways that remain influential.'[38]

Columbus monuments and statues were also under fire in the USA. Since the start of the renewed Black Lives Matter protests in 2020, some 33 of the 150 statues have been taken down (see Figure 3).[39] Although Columbus never set foot

Figure 3 Fallen Columbus statue outside the Minnesota State Capitol. St. Paul (USA) 2020. Photo Tony Webster. https://en.wikipedia.org/wiki/List_of_ monuments_and_memorials_removed_during_the_George_Floyd_protests#/ media/File:Christopher_Columbus_Statue_Torn_Down_at_Minnesota_State_ Capitol_on_June_10,_2020.jpg

---

[37] Ryback, Ellis and Glahn eds. 2021, 233–234. [38] Frei 2019.
[39] Angeleti 2020; Brito 2020.

on US soil, for Italian-Americans his statues symbolize the history of Italians in the US. One of the reasons is that in the nineteenth century, Italian immigrants had faced violent discrimination by a predominantly northern European population. In 1891, eleven Italian migrants were lynched and murdered in New Orleans. A year later, as part of an apology to Italian Americans, authorities organized celebrations for Columbus Day and supported the construction of Columbus monuments across the country well into the twentieth century. The name of Columbus is even present on Mars today. The Exploration Rover Spirit, which landed on the Red Planet in 2004, carried a plaque commemorating the Columbia crew who had died the previous year.[40] The space shuttle Columbia had disintegrated during re-entry over Texas and Louisiana, killing all seven astronauts on board. NASA had designated the landing site as Columbia Memorial Station, perpetuating the image of 'the discovery of empty space.'

Nevertheless, beginning in 1991, indigenous communities in Berkeley, California, initiated an Indigenous Peoples Day as counter-programming to celebrate the people who lived in the Americas long before the arrival of Columbus.[41] Several cities and states adopted the holiday. Former president Joe Biden endorsed the holiday with a presidential proclamation. Regarding the removal of the Columbus monuments, in 2020, Higuayagua Taíno chief Jorge Baracutei Estevez explained that it has been meaningful to see them come down: 'it's almost like a weight off my chest because it's like a validation.'[42] After centuries, indigenous peoples had gained some level of access to public spaces to tell their own stories.

In the next section, I will approach a memory landscape as a narrative to better understand how and why certain groups of people experience public spaces as exclusive, but also how these 'monumental narratives' are subject to change.

Monumental Narrativity

A landscape of memory is like a history book that is regularly updated. Some stories are told with pride and awe, others are forgotten or ignored. From this perspective the discussions and conflicts about public monuments are also a request from communities to reconfigure the book of this landscape: to add other histories or to retell the whole narrative about battles, leaders, victims, poverty, revolt, suppression, and liberation by composing a narrated past with another plot. Considering that history means making 'the absent-which-once-was' present, this request implies a recognition of other collective memories, in terms of philosopher Paul Ricoeur: to also make these present 'by the act of putting things into narrative.'[43]

---

[40] See www.nbcnews.com/id/wbna4142542.   [41] Waxman 2021.   [42] Brito 2020.
[43] Ricoeur 2016, 31.

In his narrative philosophy, Ricoeur has extensively explained how narratives reshape the human world of actions (including suffering), allowing the meaning of people's lived experiences to be understood. Inspired by Aristotle he distinguishes three interconnected stages of interpretation (imitations or *mimesis* of human actions) similar to the three literary categories: prefiguration, configuration and refiguration. Narrative is then a process of *configuring* time, i.e. the shaping of temporal aspects *prefigured* in past actions.[44] The process of configuration occurs in plots that give coherence to the narrative.[45] The plot organizes and integrates scattered events, processes, causes, motives, opportunities, and unexpected outcomes from the past into a meaningful whole, which makes the story intelligible and readable. Actors can be social movements, institutions, political leaders, thinkers, inventors, men, and women. Based on productive imagination, the configuration establishes a 'synthesis of the heterogeneous'.[46]

Ricoeur claimed that the narrative configuration of time is comparable to architecture as a configuration of space.[47] This architectural narrativity resembles the monumental narrativity of landscapes of memory. While the chronological dating of memory landscape guides people's temporal orientation, its spatiality facilitates the transition from individual experiences to a shared memory, a collective body of people who often do not know each other.[48] The landscape functions both as a facilitator and as a product of collective memory. In turn, each monument in the landscape embodies the entanglement of time and space: prefigured in past actions, it is configured in a plot – for example triumph, rivalry, sacrifice, grief, rebellion, liberation – that generates a specific point of view. Public monuments are usually surrounded by other memorials or statues that together shape the intertextuality. An important element of configuration is exactly this intertextuality: the mutual relationships of other (old and new) stories that influence readers' interpretations. In the case of landscapes it concerns the construction of, for example, heroic equestrian statues, bas-reliefs of armies, or memorials of grief as a process of inscribing in the existing landscape of memory. The network of already-there monuments and memorials contextualize and give meaning to every new monument. A memory landscape as a whole with various material markers is therefore a kind of palimpsest of time and space: a (re)mediated adapted piece of parchment on which commissioners, architects, visual artists, visitors, and tourists leave their traces.

Ricoeur's third literary category is the *refiguration* of the narrative. While reading, the reader deals with the narrative constraints and enacts the plot. Here the world of the text – or the landscape – intersects with the world of the reader,

---

[44] Ricoeur 1988, 241.   [45] Ricoeur 1984, 65–68.   [46] Ricoeur 1984, 66.
[47] Ricoeur 2004, 150; Ricoeur 2016, 31.   [48] Ambury 2006, 109.

listener or viewer where real activities take place. As Ricoeur puts it, the plot 'is completed only in the reader or in the spectator, that is to say, in the living receiver of the narrated story.'[49] An important characteristic of a plot is its endpoint which makes the story into a meaningful whole, a closure where expectation in the beginning finds its fulfilment. Because landscapes of memory are usually open-ended and its 'authors' are quite vague, the question arises whether a landscape of memory can be considered as a narrative with a plot. Is closure possible while dwelling through a urban landscape of memory with various monuments as material markers?

Memory landscapes are the outcome of changing social-political ideologies as well as the result of local or national politics of funding, marketing, debate, authorization, and reception. Following the biographical approach, landscapes are human lifeworlds: successive generations of people have (re)created and (re) appropriated places and monuments from the past, incorporating them into their collective memories and their lifeworlds in interaction with the existing landscape.[50] Every public statue, bust, or bas-relief in these landscapes is a configuration of past actions and express values such as admiration, appreciation, or warnings for the future. They can function as reminders and can support the struggle against forgetting.[51] The purposes of these monuments – e.g. to remember, to admire, or to warn – are time-bound. This implies that, in an ongoing process of distanciation and reinterpretation, walking through a landscape of memory and viewing the monuments erected decades earlier can create a sense of anachronism and alienation. After all, the composition of visitors and walkers changes over time. Then a closure becomes no longer possible for everyone and resistance may arise.

Inspired by Ricoeur, philosopher James Ambury argues that monuments acquire a certain semantic autonomy: they are cut off from the intentions of the original sculptor and the purposes of sponsors, from the initial interpretations of the public, and from the socio-cultural circumstances in which the monument was created.[52] While every monument is in that sense a time-bound micro-narrative, assembled in a specific area – park, mall, neighbourhood, city – together they can form the larger narrative of a landscape of memory. In the words of Ricoeur: 'Whether it is fixed space or space for dwelling, or space to be traversed, constructed space consists in a system of sites for the major interactions of life.'[53] However, these interactions also depend of 'the mnemonic properties' of a landscape.[54] Different narratives run through the same landscape, as different histories have been re-inscribed and reinterpreted over time. At the same time, some

---

[49] Ricoeur 1991, 26.   [50] Kolen, Renes and Hermans eds. 2015, 25.   [51] Ricoeur 2004, 41.
[52] Ambury 2006, 115.   [53] Ricoeur 2004, 150.   [54] Van Dijk 2017.

monuments can offer new ways of looking, interpreting, and revising. As walkers move through the landscape, passing iconic buildings, monuments, memorials, and other material representations, they can create and recreate their own narratives. An additional issue is that some landscapes have tangible memories with particularly 'thick meanings', such as the urban landscape of Berlin where many memorials predominantly deal with the Second World War and the Holocaust. While this urban landscape of memory emerged gradually and is accessible to everyone, the Memento Park in Budapest is a deliberately designed thematic museum with the explicit purpose to show propaganda monuments and statues from Hungary's Communist period. Visitors must purchase entrance tickets to see the statues in the park. Another, but completely accessible memory landscape is the National Mall in Washington D.C.

The National Mall in Washington

The National Mall in Washington D.C. was created in the early nineteenth century. It is an immense landscaped park with museums, memorials, sculptures and statues, covering over two hundred years of American history. The monuments of national – mostly male – heroes and events 'promise to immerse visitors in the "essential" America, the "soul of the nation".'[55] The original plan was to show the permanence of America's nation and to evoke a lasting sense of national identity. The geometric arrangement of the Mall and the classical architecture of buildings and monuments still convey authority, suggesting eternal values. The current core area lies between the American Capitol in the east and the Washington Monument in the West, which is built in the shape of an Egyptian obelisk. The obelisk was intended to evoke the timelessness of ancient civilizations. It embodies the awe, respect, and gratitude the nation felt for its most revered Founding Father, George Washington. When completed in 1885, the Washington Monument was the tallest building in the world at 555 feet (169 metre) (see Figure 4). It had surpassed the Cologne Cathedral in Germany. Other popular and frequently visited landmarks are the Lincoln Memorial, the Jefferson Memorial, the Vietnam Veterans Memorial, and Marin Luther King Jr. Memorial.

In his book *Monument Wars*, Kirk Savage historicizes the creation of the National Mall by showing the involvement of several architects, the dynamics of the changing popularity of its many monuments over time, and revealing the shift from the nineteenth-century concept of a decentralized landscape with 'ground'-heroic statues spread out in traffic circles and picturesque parks into a more controlled area with symmetric walking routes. Both critics and

---

[55] Reston 1995, quoted in Savage 2009, 10.

Figure 4 Washington Monument (Washington D.C., USA). Photo Greyfiveys. https://en.wikipedia.org/wiki/Washington_Monument#/media/File:Washington_Monument_2022.jpg

supporters of the Mall agree that the landscape of monuments around 1900 was an 'ill-defined, unplanned jumble'.[56] Originally the Mall offered meandering walks along various monuments, with trees and picturesque parks. In the 1920s and 1930s, designers began to clean up the Mall by cutting off trees, constructing and placing new monuments. Strolling along winding paths was over.[57] Yet the Mall landscape as a whole has never been fully brought under control, due to the unpredictable effects of human use and practice.

Particularly striking in this respect is what happened to the Lincoln Memorial on the Mall, unveiled in 1922. The designers had downplayed Lincoln's role in the abolition of slavery. However, in the 1960s, the Memorial became a very important anchor and tangible place in the Black Civil Rights Movement. After the election of Barack Obama as the first black American president in 2009,

---

[56] Savage 2009, 12. [57] Savage 2009, 217.

the Memorial became even more popular and visited. Savage explains how the interaction between visitors, monuments and societal circumstances makes the memorial landscape alive: the monuments not only 'retell the story of the nation but in certain times and places they change national history itself'.[58] Hence due to political and social changes in society, groups of visitors and walkers can attribute different or modified memories to the existing monuments and memorials in a landscape. In this way they construct new narratives or adapt old ones. Through this interaction, walking past iconic monuments and memorials on the National Mall, the landscape itself becomes an actor and a stage of a new collective narrative, generating an intersubjective memory experience. This process of what Ricoeur calls 'refiguration by the walker' allows for a possible closure. In sum, mnemonic change in public space is ultimately linked to the potential of monumental narrativity.

3 Monuments and Necropolitical Space

Defacing or tearing down triumphal public monuments often articulates activists' desire to change the mnemonic regime and to gain recognition for the community with which they identify. One of the reasons for such protests is that the monuments in question exude indifference to past massacres and extermination of populations, due to oppression – especially in former colonies – insurgency, war violence, and genocide. However, caring for the dead, remembering, and showing respect are important elements in the existence and continuity of any community.[59] Burial rituals connect the living with the dead and perpetuate a collective memory across generations. Mausoleums, cemeteries, monuments, and tombs are the relatively permanent markings of a social and political community. Those who do not know where their relatives and ancestors are buried, who have no material or symbolic anchors to commemorate the dead of their community, often feel displaced, denied, and dehistoricized.

This section discusses the significance of monuments for the relationship between the living and the dead, an issue much overlooked. First, I reflect on the hierarchical commemorations of the dead, particularly during both World Wars. Next, I focus on the role that monuments play in disrupting or restoring the necropolitical space, summarized as the connection between the living and the dead that holds a community together. This phenomenon will be illustrated by the destruction of ancient French royal tombs by French revolutionaries in 1793, and the current excavation and reburial of Spanish Civil War victims. Using the concept of necropolitical space, I then analyze the controversies surrounding the colonial statue of Jan Pietersz. Coen in Hoorn.

---

[58] Savage 2009, 11.   [59] Laqueur 2015.

Inequality of Monumental Memory

Reinhart Koselleck regarded the political death cult as an anthropological phenomenon, indispensable to any understanding of a culture.[60] In his research into West-European memory landscapes with a special interest in the deaths of common soldiers, he points to the irony that the Arc de Triomphe in Paris – erected in 1836 – only served to commemorate Napoleon Bonaparte's generals and victories, without paying attention to the large number of killed soldiers in the battles.[61] It was not until after the Great War, in 1921, that the Tomb of the Unknown Soldier was placed beneath the Arc in recognition of those who carried out the actual fighting. It is nevertheless remarkable that in 1971, as a tribute, sixteen larger-than-life statues of French generals and marshals from the First Empire, the Franco-Prussian War and the First World War were placed at the foot of the Verdun Citadel. Originally a gift from Minister André Malraux to the Louvre, the statues were too colossal for the museum. Today, along the so-called Crossroads of the Marshals as a parade of war heroes, nothing reminds passers-by of the millions of other dead: soldiers, doctors, nurses, and civilians.[62]

The Unknown Soldier or Unknown Warrior, referring to all who lost their lives often without a trace on the bloody battlefields, became a symbolic figure in which the memory of the nation was united.[63] The new public memorial supported the modern nation-state with meaningful prestige. It potentially assured all its citizens of a framework with which to identify, giving them a sense of belonging to a greater whole. Along with other memorials, the Unknown Soldier gave the message that the sacrifice of men had not been in vain: they had died for the higher purpose of the 'Fatherland'. The Tomb of the Unknown Soldier became a central place of national worship: 'The Altar of the Fatherland'.[64] This symbolism hardly applied to soldiers from the colonies, though millions of mobilized African and Asian men had fought in the First World War,[65] nor to women who worked in military hospitals or munitions factories, or those who were victims of sexual war violence.[66] Women were remembered as grieving mothers, mourning the loss of their sons and husbands. In France and Belgium, for example, several First World War monuments feature a grieving mother, reminiscent of the Renaissance Pietà.[67]

Historian Thomas Laqueur describes in his book *The Work of the Dead* the initial doubts of the English political elite – especially the Archbishop of Canterbury and the King – about the idea of burying the anonymous corpse of a common soldier in

---

[60] Koselleck 1994, 9. [61] Koselleck 2023, 110. [62] Grever 2024, 148.
[63] Anderson 1983, 9. [64] Mosse 1990, 93. [65] Rigney 2021, 11.
[66] Assmann 2006, 73–74; Grever 2018, 33–34.
[67] E.g. www.tracesofwar.com/sights/132856/Sculpture-Grieving-Mother-Belgian-War-Cemetery-Keiem.htm.

Westminster Abbey. But the resonance proved staggering. On 11 November in 1920 – simultaneously with the interment of the French Unknown Soldier in Paris – the burial ceremony evoked intense emotions (see Figures 5 and 6). More than a million and a quarter people slowly walked past the grave in the Abbey.[68]

Koselleck argued that since the technical mass destruction in the First World War, in some areas of the battles, the number of no longer identifiable or completely missing bodies exceeded the number of those who could still find

Figure 5 Coffin of the Unknown Warrior in Westminster Abbey before burial. London (UK) 1920. Photo Horace Nicholls. https://en.wikipedia.org/wiki/ The_Unknown_Warrior#/media/File:The_Unknown_Warrior_at_ Westminster_Abbey,_November_1920_Q31514.jpg

---

[68] Laqueur 2015, 479–481.

Figure 6 Tomb of the Unknown Warrior in Westminster Abbey. Photo Mike. https://en.wikipedia.org/wiki/The_Unknown_Warrior

their grave. Mass graves and 'comrade graves' became a kind of memorial *sui generis*.[69] And the hundreds of thousands missing received their own special large monuments on which their names could now be recorded, an attempt to rescue each vanished individual.

The Great War had stimulated a different way of dealing with the remains of unthinkably large numbers of fallen soldiers, also because many bodies had been torn to pieces. It was often impossible to ascribe an identity or even a nationality to corpses and body parts found scattered across the battlefields. Permanent cemeteries were established with thousands of graves. The National Cemetery of Fleury-devant-Douaumont, for example, contains the remains of French soldiers killed in the fighting that took place in the Verdun area from 1914 to 1918, in particular the horrific Battle of Verdun in 1916. In the years that followed, as more and more bodies were discovered, they were buried marked by a Christian cross; more than half of these were eventually identified. The Douaumont Ossuary, officially opened on 23 June 1929, dominates the cemetery. The building consists of a 137-metre-long cloister, with recesses housing 46 tombs containing the bones of 130,000 French and German soldiers. Above the main porch stands a 'Tower of the Dead' in the form of a lighthouse whose rotating beam illuminates the former battlefield. Close to the cemetery are two other public monuments. One, erected in 1938, dedicated to all Jewish soldiers who fell for France in the First World War, and the other in memory of 28,000

---

[69] Koselleck 2023, 84.

Muslim soldiers unveiled much later, in 2006, by President Jacques Chirac. This public memorial was the first to Muslims who died of the clashes over the strategically located Verdun and in other First World War battles.[70] A few more memorials to soldiers from the colonies had been erected. One of the earliest is dedicated to Afro-American troops in Monthois (Ardennes) in France, in 1919. The monument – a small pillar – is a lasting tribute to the sacrifice of the 372nd Infantry, and all African American troops who saw combat in the First World War. These memorials and monuments express respect but at the same time perpetuate racial divisions and the exclusion of 'foreign bodies'.[71]

Britain and France also imported workers from their colonies to work behind the front lines. The largest group came from China, that is, mostly poor farmers from the northern provinces of Shandong and Hebei.[72] Between 1916 and 1918, some 140,000 Chinese workers from the Chinese Labour Corps, travelled via Canada to Europe and risked their lives building roads, digging trenches in the battlefields and removing corpses of dead soldiers. It was dirty but vital and dangerous work, often behind the lines on the Western Front, never really recognized and quickly forgotten. Many of the workers never returned home. In France and Belgium, Commonwealth cemeteries with Chinese graves of so-called 'Unsung Heroes of World War I' were established in 1921 and are maintained to this day (see Figure 7).[73] It took almost a century for monuments and statues to be erected to the Chinese workers, for example in 2017 in Poperinge and in 2018 in Paris.[74] In the United Kingdom in 2017, Chinese labourers – known as 'the forgotten of the forgotten' – were commemorated for the first time for their efforts in the First World War. Wreaths were laid at the Cenotaph in London. In 2018, the British Embassy in Beijing donated a plaque honouring the contribution of the Chinese Labour Corps in Qingdao in the Shandong Province.[75]

After the Second World War, fallen soldiers from the colonies and American black soldiers similarly received little attention, care and respect. About 250,000 North-African soldiers had fought in the French army, mainly Algerians, Tunisians, and Moroccans; the US sent 1.2 million African Americans into the war in an army almost completely segregated by race.[76]

---

[70] See www.tracesofwar.com/sights/43123/Memroial-Jewish-Soldiers-Verdun.htm and www.tracesofwar.com/sights/43121/Memorial-Muslim-Soldiers.htm.
[71] Rigney 2021, 11.   [72] Xu 2011; Bailey 2018.
[73] See www.chinastory.cn/ywdbk/english/v1/detail/20190627/10127000000427415616029331 15843977_1.html.
[74] See www.ww1cemeteries.com/bel-chinese-labour-corps-memorial-poperinge.html and www .xinhuanet.com/english/2018-09/21/c_137482830.htm.
[75] See www.gov.uk/government/news/uk-plaque-unveiled-honouring-the-chinese-labour-corps.
[76] Ferrell 2011; Amatmoekrim 2018.

Figure 7 Entrance to the Chinese cemetery in Noyelles-sur-Mer (France). Photo Félix Potuit. https://commons.wikimedia.org/wiki/File:Cimeti%C3%A8re_chinois_Noyelles_2007_1.jpg

Public memorials were not or much later erected for them and often not on central locations. Black soldiers often buried the bodies of their white comrades. For example, the American cemetery in the Dutch village Margraten (Limburg), where 19,000 people were (temporarily) buried, was constructed by black Americans. One exception is the U.S. Memorial Wereth, erected in 1994 on a private initiative. It is a tribute to eleven arrested African American soldiers of the 333rd U.S. Field Artillery Battalion who were brutally murdered by the SS. In 2002, the non-profit organization 'U.S. Wereth Memorial' was founded, which purchased the land around the memorial stone and had a more extensive monument inaugurated there in 2004. It commemorates not only the Eleven of Wereth but also all African American soldiers who were active in Europe.[77]

---

[77] See https://wereth.org/en/home-2/.

Similar to Koselleck, Laqueur emphasizes that no culture is indifferent to human remains: 'dead bodies matter'.[78] Honouring and mourning the dead fulfil an existential function for the living as they connect past, present, and future. The Geneva Conventions of 1929 and 1949 therefore provided that those who die in war have the right to a dignified burial and that the dead should, if possible, be buried according to the rites of the religion to which they belonged.[79] Even in the current war between Russia and Ukraine, both countries are making efforts to exchange killed soldiers so that they can be buried in their home countries.

Necropolitical Space

How the living deal with the dead reveals the hierarchies of a community, including the possibilities for continuing old alliances and forging new ones.[80] While Laqueur views this relationship as an imagined shared community, philosopher Hans Ruin argues that the living not only look after human remains and bones, but also relate to the dead in a concrete way: humans live with the living and with the dead. In his book *Being with the Dead* Ruin introduces the concept of necropolitical space, the space that is 'constituted and upheld by both the living and the dead'.[81] The organization of public funerals with recurring memorial rituals, the erection of monuments and the creation of a mental legacy help shape the political space of a community, bringing the living and the dead together in a social bond across generations.

Hence the dead are important in the establishment and maintenance of political communities. Allowing their voices to be taken into account is a sign of recognition and respect. All these actions are not only about remembering and commemorating, but also about the question of who counts in commemorating the dead, and how and when this happens. The mutual relationship of the living and the dead of a community form a larger sociality as a figurative space of the *historical*. In the ongoing human connection with the dead a sense of 'pastness' emerges. Caring for the dead can instil in people a sense of historicity: the awareness of the historical situatedness of being-in-the-world. The dead are not merely non-beings but appear in the memories of the living as a 'positive continuation of life'.[82] The condition of being with the dead draws human beings out of themselves into an intersubjective temporal space that they share with others. Commemorating the dead also sustains ancestral relations or 'ancestrality'. Whereas funeral rites relate to human remains, ancestrality focuses on how the living worship and communicate with the dead. This is

---

[78] Laqueur 2015, 1 and 82. [79] Petrig 2009. [80] Oestigaard and Goldhahn, 2006.
[81] Ruin 2018, 7. [82] Ruin 2018, 17. Parts of this section are also based on Grever 2025B.

not some kind of primitive cult of the dead, Ruin argues, but a 'general condition and dimension of human historicity'.[83]

This philosophy echoes what Hannah Arendt stated years ago in *The Human Condition*: the common world consists of people with whom we live and with those who came before us and those who will come after us. The common world can survive to the extent that it appears in public and transcends the limited lifespan of mortal men. Referring to classical antiquity, Arendt claimed that the curse of slavery at the time not only consisted in being deprived of freedom and of visibility, but also in the fear of these people themselves 'that from being obscure they should pass away leaving no trace that they have existed'.[84] That is why anonymous mass graves are so disturbing: they show indifference to the dehumanized dead. After the Holocaust, scholars underscored the urgency of a public monument precisely because nameless millions were murdered.[85] A monument refers to the life that people once lived and affirms the appreciation and affection of the deceased in the present. Taking their voices into account is a moral responsibility for every community.

The relationship and interaction between the living and the dead can continue and change over time, but it can also be disrupted or broken. There are several historical examples of how the necropolitical space can be modified, erased or restored. The unearthing and reburial of dead bodies particularly play an important role during regimes changes.

Ruin points to a striking example of how French revolutionaries in 1793 destroyed the centuries-old royal tombs of the French kings in the mausoleum of the basilica in Saint-Denis near Paris. In his view the purpose of this iconoclasm on behalf of the new government – the 'second killing' of the dead kings – was to create a new necropolitical space.[86] The coffins were opened with picks and crowbars. The embalmed or mummified bodies – if intact – were then displayed and dismembered for days on end. Some exhumed corpses caused sensation and awe, such as the still intact corpses of King Henri IV and general Vicomte de Turenne. This last corpse was the only one the revolutionaries spared for his deep bond to his soldiers. All others were torn into pieces and dumped in a trench. Even the dead did not escape the revolutionary violence. The operations had to symbolically consolidate the new regime of the French Republic. According to France's National Convention it was 'the Last Judgment of kings'.[87] In this way the revolutionaries hoped to create a rupture in France's necropolitical space.

More than two centuries later, a radical transformation of the necropolitical space is taken place in Spain. In 2019, the government led by Pedro Sánchez

---

[83] Ruin 2018, 82–83. [84] Arendt 1958, 55. [85] Huyssen 1994. [86] Ruin 2018, 90.
[87] Lindsay 2015.

moved the embalmed body of dictator Francisco Franco from the crypt church of Spain's most contested national monument in the Valle de Cuelgamuros – formerly called the Valley of the Fallen – to a less prominent cemetery north of Madrid. This was soon followed by the removal of the body of José Antonio Primo de Rivera, founder of the Fascist Falange Movement in 1933.[88] The government currently considers what to do with the monument: a gigantic crypt church (basilica) with a Benedictine abbey, a guest house and four cylindrical sixteenth century monoliths (see Figure 8). Proposals range from functional reclassification, building a counter-monument to total destruction.

There is also another reason why this monument is so controversial. It turned out that hidden behind the side chapels of the church, the skeletons of thousands

Figure 8 Franco monument in the Valle de Cuelgamuros (Spain). Photo Håkan Svensson. https://commons.wikimedia.org/wiki/File:ValleDeLosCaidos_Cross_north_side1.jpg

---

[88] See www.theguardian.com/world/2023/apr/23/body-of-spains-fascist-party-founder-to-be-removed-from-basilica.

of anonymous citizens and Republican fighters were dumped to fill the mausoleum. The Franco regime had mass graves and personal graves emptied without the knowledge and approval of family members.[89] To this day, relatives of republicans fight to get the remains of their relatives out of this monument, which for them is a glorification of fascism.

The National Monument is a reminder of the Pact of Silence, the silent agreement between Francoist-reformist and moderate political parties to grant general amnesty for the crimes committed during Franco's dictatorship.[90] After decades of political consensus about forgetting the past, the Pact is now crumbling and with it the legitimacy of the monument. Across Spain, human bones are now lifted from anonymity using a combination of modern DNA testing and ancestral memory.[91] Spaniards are digging for the disappeared, trying to find the remains of murdered people to rebury them. It seems an uprising of skeletons: at least 740 mass graves have been opened; 9,000 bodies reburied. Once the identification of the remains has been completed, it may be possible for the bereaved to come to some closure and memorials can be erected.[92] But restoring a necropolitical space does not always succeed.

Monuments as Colonial Aphasia: the Banda Massacre

For a long time, the dominant idea among the Dutch was that the Netherlands has historically been a tolerant and ethical nation. After the Second World War and the independence of the colonies, Dutch culture was characterized by a denial of racial discrimination and colonial violence. Racism seemed an American phenomenon. Plantations with enslaved people in the eighteenth and nineteenth centuries were located in the southern states of the US, not in the Dutch colonies.[93] Within the academic field of history at Dutch universities, colonial history – focused on the Dutch East Indies – was a separate field of historiography and hardly related to the history of the 'Fatherland'. Most Dutch historians ignored the fact that national identity was constructed in times of violent conquest and colonial exploitation.[94] Denial also regarded colonial statues, monuments, façade stones, and street names. In the eyes of many, these monuments referred to a distant past that they no longer had anything to do with. That some representations could be painful for Dutch people with colonial roots from former Dutch colonies – Suriname, the Antilles, Indonesia – others did not see or did not want to see.

Philomena Essed and Isabel Hoving consider this attitude as 'smug ignorance'.[95] This striking designation resembles what Ann Stoler describes in

---

[89] Grever 2025B, 8.   [90] Driessen 2013, 41; Matteo 2023.
[91] Wildeboer Schut and Dujisin 2022.   [92] Driessen 2013, 43–44.
[93] Van Stipriaan 2007, 205.   [94] Grever and Legêne 2024, 33.   [95] Essed and Hoving 2014.

the context of French colonial historiography as 'colonial aphasia'. The term aphasia includes forgetting or amnesia, but above all a loss of access and active dissociation. Stoler points to a blockage of knowledge, a dismembering, and a difficulty of retrieving conceptual and lexical vocabularies.[96] In the field of speech and language research, aphasia refers to a range of impairments in language after a brain damage.[97] It means a language disorder in which, for example, no words can be found for an object or in which visual perception cannot be adequately translated into language. This approach may shed more light on the resistance to moving a statue of a man who, even by seventeenth-century standards, committed extreme violence in the Dutch colonies: the statue of Jan Pieterszoon Coen, placed on the central square of his hometown Hoorn in 1893.

Coen, trained as a merchant and charged with a political-military task, became the fourth Governor-General of the Dutch East India Company (VOC) in the early seventeenth century. He expelled the Portuguese from the Solor archipelago, prevented interference by the Spanish and the English, and treated the local population extremely cruelly.[98] Although the States General, Prince Maurits of Orange and the VOC-board sometimes expressed their disapproval of the excessive violence, they nevertheless agreed with his actions, not least because it yielded much wealth. The result was the establishment of the extensive colonial empire of the Dutch Republic in the East Indies.

In 1619, Coen destroyed the city of Jakarta and established the military and administrative headquarters of the VOC on its remains, which was henceforth called Batavia.[99] Two years later he organized a military expedition to Banda Lontor (today Banda Besar), the largest of the seven volcanic Banda Islands in the Moluccas. The aim was to gain complete control over the trade and cultivation of nutmeg, a very rare and sought-after spice. For a long time, Banda was the only place on earth were the nutmeg tree grew.[100] In their quest for a Dutch monopoly, Coen and his men subdued Lontor and killed over 14,000 Bandanese, culminating in the massacre on 8 May, 1621. Some survivors were enslaved and deported to Batavia, their villages burned down. Others managed to escape to Seram north of the Banda Islands.[101] Forty-four village leaders (*Orang Kaya*) were interrogated under torture on Banda Neira and beheaded by Japanese samurai executioners in the service of the VOC. They mutilated their bodies and impaled the heads on bamboo sticks to be shown in public.[102] At the instigation of the VOC, Coen and his ship's council had decided to depopulate the island; later they repopulated the island with prisoners and enslaved people.[103]

---

[96] Stoler 2011, 122 and 125.   [97] Code and Petheram 2011.
[98] Van Goor 2015, 361; Van Engelenhoven 2022, 81–82.   [99] Van Goor 2015, 363–368, 376.
[100] Ghosh 2021, 21–30.   [101] Colenbrander 1919, 742; Heuser 2023, 23.
[102] Van Goor 2015, 455–457; Van Donkersgoed, 2023, 510.   [103] Loth 1995.

Despite this extreme violence – *genocide* according to the 1946 UN Convention – the Dutch romanticized the nutmeg production from the nineteenth century onwards. With the rise of nationalism in the 1880s, the political elite – including the Minister of the Colonies and Queen Wilhelmina – promoted Coen as a Dutch national hero. Dissenting voices were – sometimes explicitly – suppressed, negatively framed, or ignored. Coen became ubiquitous and visible in the Netherlands through schoolbooks and wall charts, museum exhibitions and various public physical representations. In addition to the statue in Hoorn, for example, many cities named streets, squares, boats, and bridges after him. The glorification supported the Dutch narrative template of a small country with a large colonial empire. Unlike the United Kingdom, the formation of the Dutch nation-state took place in a period of decline. The period of the mighty Republic was over; in the 1830s, the southern part of the Netherlands turned into independent Belgium. The new but small Dutch kingdom meant little on the international political stage, except for its 'overseas colonial possessions'. National awareness was characterized by hurt national feelings and nostalgia, 'a secret longing for the lost grandeur' of a Golden Age.[104] This self-image has changed, but its echo is still present in the Netherlands.

Nevertheless, already in the 1860s, historians, writers and journalists criticized plans to erect a statue of Coen both in Batavia and Hoorn. Critical voices have been continued throughout the twentieth century to this day by historians, (play)writers, politicians, and activists, including Moluccan Dutch related to descendants of the Bandanese survivors. In the 1960s and 1970s, the statue in Hoorn was regularly smeared and slogans such as 'Get it down' were painted on the plinth. In 1987 a dramatic protest took place.

On the occasion of the commemoration of Coen's 400th birthday, the local Westfries Museum organized the exhibition: 'J.P. Coen, deeds and days in the service of the VOC'. At the official opening, the invited Moluccan Dutch artist Willy Nanlohy – dressed as Alfoer, according to myths the progenitor of the Moluccan people – presented Queen Beatrix's Prince consort Claus with a 'black book' describing Coen's gruesome misdeeds (see Figure 9). He then left the room in silence. After this, activists distributed leaflets explaining Nanlohy's action, only to be quickly confiscated by security guards. The dignitaries and other attendees became agitated, except for Prince Claus. Sensitive to discrimination and interested in cultures outside Europe, he was the only one who remained calm.[105]

The reason for this action was that Nanlohy felt closely related to his brothers on the Banda islands in the Moluccas, where his grandfather originally came

---

[104] Blaas 2000, 13; Oostindie 2011, 7; Grever and Legêne 2023, 30.   [105] Steijlen 2015.

Figure 9 Artist Nanlohy presented Prince Claus with a 'black book' about Coen's atrocities on Banda. Hoorn (Netherlands) 1987. Photo Rob C. Croes (copy right Nationaal Archief). https://www.nationaalarchief.nl/onderzoeken/fotocollectie/ad605ef4-d0b4-102d-bcf8-003048976d84

from. He was shocked on discovering Coen's glorification and felt used. As a sign of protest and mourning, he had also covered his sculptures installed for the exhibition with black cloths.[106] Most of these protests and other actions have been written out of history. In 2003, a memorial had been erected on Banda Neira around the Parigi Rante well. Initiator was the late Indonesian historian Des Alwi (1927–2010) who was born on that island. On a plaque visitors can read what happened in 1621 with the names of the executed *Orang Kayas* and the villages where they came from.[107]

In 2012, an updated text with critical comments was added to the plinth. But that did not stop the resistance. An explanatory text cannot avoid the impression that the posture of this statue conceals colonial violence. Controversy flared up

---

[106] Steijlen 2018, 1–3.   [107] See https://pala.westfriesmuseum.nl/echo/echo-article/?lang=en.

Figure 10 Mobile police protects statue of J.P. Coen from protesters. Hoorn (Netherlands) 2020. Photo Benno Ellerbroek.

due to global postcolonial movements, Black Lives Matter in particular. On 13 June, 2020, the leader of the radical right-wing political party Forum for Democracy laid flowers at Coen's statue as a sign of admiration.[108] The gesture was both political propaganda and a form of re-appropriation. Six days later, things started to get going. Activists pro and contra the statue demonstrated. Serious disturbances broke out. The mobile police kept opposing groups in line with great difficulty (see Figure 10).

Defenders of the statue consider Coen a hero.[109] For them, the actions are an attack on Hoorn and the Netherlands. They show, in Stoler's terms, colonial aphasia: a lack of understanding for the Banda massacre and the impact of four hundred years of Dutch colonial exploitation, neither do they understand how colonial violence resonates through monuments.[110] There is a double standard here: certain dead are important and belong to *us*, other dead belong to *them*, those far away. To paraphrase Laqueur: some bodies matter and others don't or not as much, especially if they are black.

Interestingly, during the corona pandemic in 2020–2021, shortly after the demonstrations and counter-demonstrations in Hoorn, the Westfries Museum set up the online exhibition *Pala, Nutmeg Tales of Banda*. In order to contextualize the Banda massacre from different perspectives, the museum invited scholars and activists to join the editorial board. Because the exhibition had to be online,

---

[108] Van der Vlies 2024, 223.   [109] Grever 2025A, 384–385.
[110] Prescott and Lahti 2022, 465.

boundaries were crossed and people from all over the world were involved, including Moluccan scholars from Indonesia.[111] Based on dialogue, exchange, and evidence, the group co-created a special exhibition with an impressive amount of – partly new – knowledge about the complex history of Banda: their long legendary pre-colonial past, their rich culture, their dealings with various traders and their resistance to the colonial violence by Coen and the VOC.

Then, on 8 May, 2021, the municipality of Hoorn received a letter from Bandanese descendants in Indonesia. It is a powerful statement of protest. The Bandanese declared Coen's hero worship unacceptable and request the statue's removal, because of the atrocities committed by the Dutch to enforce a monopoly over the nutmeg production: 'taking more than fourteen thousand human lives by murderous slaughter and starvation together with large scale persecution and expulsion from our ancestral land and depriving us from our Heritage, including our Economic, Cultural heritage, Language and Religion.' The writers considered this violence an act of 'Crimes Against Humanity, as GENOCIDE', and ended the statement: 'Thus, we present for consideration with respect to Universal Human Rights and the rightful grievances of the progeny of the ancestors of WANDAN.'[112]

The letter was sent via the Building the Baileo foundation. This foundation, consisting of Moluccans from second to fifth generation evacuated migrants in the Netherlands in 1951, keeps the original Moluccan culture alive, using songs, music, dance, and stories.[113] They had reached out to the Bandanese in the Moluccas, which led to an online meeting in May 2021. The Bandanese talked about their history and explained their discontent about the statue of Coen. Immediately after, an official protest was sent to the Municipal Council and the Board of Mayor and Aldermen in Hoorn.[114] The background of this initiative may have been the contacts between the curators of the Pala exhibition and the Moluccans in Indonesia.

Two years later, an extensive historical report commissioned by the municipality was published.[115] It turned out that Hoorn was one of the few Dutch cities permanently represented with seven directors in the central board of the VOC, the so-called VOC-chamber Hoorn. For many years, administrators, civil servants, craftsmen and other inhabitants of Hoorn benefited financially and economically from slavery on the Banda islands and the trade of enslaved people from Asian countries and the African continent to Banda and Batavia. Later, in the eighteenth century, some inhabitants of Hoorn were also owners of

---

[111] Colophon https://pala.wfm.nl/colofon/?lang=en.   [112] Grever 2025B, 18.
[113] About the Moluccan community in the Netherlands (approx. 80,000 people), Manuhutu, Pattipeilohy and Timisela eds., 2021.
[114] Grever 2025B, 18.   [115] Heuser 2023, 25.

coffee plantations in northern South-America, such as in Berbice (Guyana). There, enslaved people were branded with the coat of arms of Hoorn.[116]

After various debates, including on this report, a majority of the Hoorn municipal council refused to apologize for its slavery past, as several other Dutch cities had done. Nor was there any official recognition of that horrific past, such as a public monument in memory of the victims of the murdered Bandanese and of Hoorn's involvement in the slave trade. This is remarkable because former Prime Minister Mark Rutte and King Willem-Alexander had shortly before apologized for the Dutch slave trade and the slavery system. This is notable for another reason as well.

Several perpetrators of colonial violence, such as J.P. Coen, have exterminated populations and their cultures. Unlike the Second World War and the Holocaust, hardly any monuments have been erected by former colonial powers in their home countries to commemorate and acknowledge the mass murders that took place under their responsibility in the colonies. One of the few exceptions is the Namibian Genocide Memorial in Bremen (Germany), commemorating the genocide of tens of thousands of Herero and Nama between 1904 and 1908 by the Germans. It concerns the rededication of the ten-metre high 'Kolonialelefant' that originally celebrated the German colonial conquests in Africa.[117] Since 1988, an explanatory board has provided a history of German colonialism. It also highlights the reason for its rededication: 'This monument is a symbol of the responsibility we have inherited from history.'[118] There is also a modest counter-memorial near the Elephant, unveiled in 2009, consisting of rocks from the Omaheke Desert in Namibia.

Trans-Cultural Understanding of Ancestral Relations

In Hoorn, Coen's statue must remain on the same square to this day; moving it to a less prominent location, as a minority of city council members and activists wanted, is not permitted. This outcome raises several ethical issues. Firstly, it shows a lack of institutional responsibility for the brutal violence that was committed at the time – justified by the VOC-chamber Hoorn – and its consequences over generations. In terms of Michael Rothberg: Hoorn obviously does not acknowledge its historically implicated position.[119] Secondly, the refusal to apologize corroborates disrespect for the 14,000 indigenous people who were killed by the Dutch in Banda in 1621. In doing so, the city council not only

---

[116] Heuser 2023, 32–33.
[117] The 'Reichskolonialehrendenkmal' (1932) was a symbol of German colonial ambition that spanned the Nazi-era and post-war reconstruction. See www.rosalux.de/en/news/id/40882/decolonising-bremen.
[118] Binter ed. 2017, 23.   [119] Rothberg 2019.

ignores the sad legacy of historical injustice, but also fails to understand the significance of the dead and the ancestors to the Bandanese community.

Yet the protests against the hero-worship of Coen can also be interpreted as an attempt to restore the broken relationship with the dead in the Bandanese community, including those living in the Netherlands. The aforementioned letter of protest from the Wandan (Bandanese) people in 2021 is evidence of this. The writers lament the killing of 'more than fourteen-thousand human lives' – dumped anonymously – and their 'expulsion from our ancestral land and depriving us from our Heritage'. They strive for recognition from their community and ancestors. The disguise as Alfoer at the opening of the Coen exhibition in 1987, by the Moluccan Dutch artist Nanlohy, also linked his protest with the Banda ancestors.[120] Nanlohy's performance briefly brought the Bandanese, who had been silenced four hundred years ago, back to life. Hence, the failure on the part of the Hoorn city council to explicitly acknowledge the massacre on Banda, the enslavement of survivors and the destruction of their lands and culture by the Dutch, is also a failure to acknowledge the meaning of the dead in the maintenance of a community. Following Ruin's argument, I therefore view the protests of Bandanese (Moluccan) descendants within the Dutch protest movement as an attempt to transform the memory landscape in Hoorn and to create a new necropolitical space 'rooted in ancestrality and being with the dead'.[121]

Obviously, the spatial and temporal differences between the three violent cases are enormous. The massacre on Banda and the destruction of lands led by Coen took place 17,000 km away in the seventeenth century, ten generations ago. The terror was perpetrated by a foreign authority mainly for economic reasons. The violence in revolutionary France and in Spain happened in the eighteenth and twentieth century, four to five generations ago. In France, the revolutionaries removed the dead kings from their graves to 'punish' them for the harsh oppression for which they had been responsible in their eyes. In Spain, the search for the murdered Republican fighters and their possible reburial is currently the focus. The bloody internal wars, which arose for political and economic reasons, divided both countries. Nevertheless, the great involvement and perhaps obsession with the dead is remarkable in the three cases. But the way in which anonymous deaths are dealt with in contemporary Spanish and Bandanese communities is more similar, despite the spatial and temporal distance between the descendants and the large-scale violence perpetrated at the time. How can we understand this?

For the Spanish and the Bandanese, the recognition of their community is important, but also the possibility of reconnecting with the dead in a reciprocal

---

[120] Steijlen 2018, 7.   [121] Ruin 2018, 90–91.

relationship within the necropolitical space. The goal for both communities is mnemonic change and recognition: to overcome oblivion and cultural disorientation by proving the existence of their culture. In that sense the distance is not that great, because both communities still maintain a lively *engagement* with their ancestors. The Bandanese – also in the diasporas – have explicitly cultivated the bond with the ancestors across generations. The massacre of 1621 is a traumatic part of their history, but the stories highlight the resistance and strength of the *Orang Kayas*.[122] Especially after the fall of President Suharto's regime in 1998, there was a cultural revival of indigenous communities such as in the Moluccas. Currently, on the Kei islands, the inhabitants have a flourishing oral tradition, also reflected in the *onotani*, songs that important women sing to commemorate their culture and ancestors.[123]

For the Bandanese descendants in the Netherlands, the triumphant statue of Coen in Hoorn justifies colonial violence in the past. In doing so, the statue not only perpetuates a culture of selective remembrance, it also allows the dead to haunt the present. Unlike modern-day Spaniards who seek out the remains of their killed relatives from the Civil War, the Bandanese cannot locate, identify, let alone rebury their dead. That tragedy happened too long ago. There are no bodily remains or hardly any other traces left. There are therefore no bones that can be returned to formerly colonized communities as a form of reparation.[124]

The dead, who confront the living with the transience of human existence, are always dependent on the living for care and respect, even generations later. Traumatic events that took place centuries ago, such as a massacre, can be experienced as present time by descendants and relatives. But ancestor worship is not necessarily tied to physical remains or burial sites; it is a socio-cultural practice of how the living of a community interact with their dead. Ruin's plea for a trans-cultural understanding of ancestrality implies an existential-ontological position of being with the dead. It also deconstructs the colonialist distinction between the irrational spiritual cult of ancestor worship versus the secular philosophical rationality in dealing with the dead.[125] Ignoring the dead and the ancestors of a community results in the denial of its existence, including its members' rights, traditions, and culture. It also prevents a sense of historicity for all involved, which can lead to continued indifference and exclusion. Perhaps a public monument commemorating the Banda massacre near Coen's statue in Hoorn offers an opportunity to integrate Dutch and Bandanese history into a *shared* social space. Such a monument could compensate for the colonial aphasia in Hoorn, at the same time granting the victims some posthumous

---

[122] Van Donkersgoed 2023, 509–510.
[123] See https://pala.westfriesmuseum.nl/echo/echo-article/?lang=en.
[124] See for instance Rassool 2015.   [125] Ruin 2018, 82–83; Laqueur 2015, 43–44.

dignity.[126] In that case, the anonymous dead will have a symbolic and visible legacy for the descendants that can testify to 'what has been'. A striking visible marker that gives recognition and humanity to the Bandanese dead might also restore the necropolitical space, the social bond between the dead and the living that holds their community together. In this way, this past can be connected to the present and the future. Subsequently, prevailing narratives about Dutch colonialism can be questioned more extensively, which offers the possibility for a new mnemonic regime.[127]

4 Iconography, Visual Language, and Multiplication

A major source of conflict surrounding public monuments is their design – iconography, style, form, materials used – and their specific place within memory landscapes with the goal, for example to honour leaders and ancestors as a form of political propaganda, to commemorate specific histories, or to offer comfort to relatives. Usually, the intended meaning is transformed into an aesthetically shaped object with a specific size and visual language, related to some socio-political function. Depending on the commissioners and the artists involved, a design conveys messages and ideologies that evoke emotions, such as empathy, recognition, respect, awe, nostalgia, or disorientation. Because such monuments indicate what communities find memorable, design, sheer size, and location are crucial to creating public visibility. The multiplication of monuments dedicated to the same person is a sign of hegemonic power. At the same time, public material representations can contain visual messages that are overlooked by some but noticed by others, provoking fear or anger. These emotions can lead to destructive actions of mutilation and damage, in sum to iconoclasm as a form of censorship.[128] Damaging or destroying a public monument not only acknowledges the seductiveness of the work, admitting that what should have no power in fact does, it also makes a hated person or event temporarily more present in public debates.[129]

This section discusses the design and multiplication of public monuments of Queen Victoria around the world, focusing on its hegemonic presence, but also on the various forms of vandalism and destruction. This is followed by an in-depth visual analysis of colonial statues of missionaries with indigenous people in various countries and continents. Then, related to Section 2, I will discuss how location and relocation of a statue or monument can cause much unrest and controversy. This will be demonstrated by the example of the Stolpersteine (stumbling stones) in Europe, which commemorate the victims of Nazi extermination, and a Second World War memorial commemorating the Soviet

---

[126] De Baets 2023.   [127] Rigney 2022.   [128] Freedberg 2016, 67.   [129] Freedberg 2016, 68.

'liberators' in the Estonian capital Tallinn. The section ends with the issue about the limits of representing atrocities of war and genocide, and the shift to more abstract, aniconic monuments.

Decline of Hegemonic Presence: Queen Victoria

The visual language of sculptural constructions often has a multi-layered history with diverse meanings for different groups. Monuments, statues and other structures in the public space are visible artistic expressions of a nation, region, or other community that can become the focus of contestation in times of political-social transition, changing demographics, and emerging awareness of historic injustices. Public monuments represent and continue a selective interpretation of past figures, events, and phenomena that finds a permanent and seemingly unchanging expression in wood, stone, marble, metal, plastic, and other materials. Statues placed on high columns or pedestals underline the perceived significance of the historical figure. When trying to understand a monument or statue, it is also important to consider the historical context, including the available techniques at the time. Different communities may view the importance of a figure or event depicted in a statue differently, but such perceptions are greatly enhanced or mitigated through their physical form and their location.

In Western countries, many monuments and memorials contain classical elements and Christian symbols with biblical quotations. This is the case, for example, with war memorials from the First World War (see Section 3). Artists used symbols that were important to the military community and recognizable to the relatives of dead soldiers, such as broken columns, obelisks, lions, eagles, and Christian crosses.[130] In contrast, the memorial to the 30,000 Muslim combatants who fell in the same war has a completely different style: built in a white painted Moorish style with Muslim inscriptions.

Perhaps crucial is the exact location in the memory landscape of a city or village. A statue or monument on a prominent square or at the entrance of a public building expresses a certain appreciation and can elicit various positive and negative reactions from the public. A protected public space with statues, busts and monuments, such as a museum park, seems less likely to lead to criticism and disputes because more context is often provided. Yet Scates and Yu argue that museum parks are not neutral spaces because they express their own politics and ideologies.[131] In general, however, the more prominently a monument is placed in public space, the greater the chance of conflicts surrounding it. This is especially true if it concerns an already controversial

---

[130] Kerby et al. 2021, 16. [131] Scates and Yu 2022. 505.

figure or event. The visualization may be offensive or shocking to people who have become increasingly negative about it over time. They may then take action and damage or destroy the statue or monument. These iconoclasts aim to ensure that 'what is dead has no chance of revival, whether in body or in spirit', showing that the image ultimately does not possess powers that transcend the material.[132]

This has happened with monuments to Queen Victoria throughout the British Empire. Especially after her golden and diamond jubilee in 1887 and 1897, the Queen's images could be seen all over the world. Honoured in central squares and parks of many cities, such as London, Dublin, Montreal, Cape Town, Calcutta, Rangoon, Lahore, Sri-Lanka, and Kingston, she was sculpted as the omnipotent dignified Great White Mother holding in her hands the regalia crown, sceptre and orb. Victoria's reign seemed imposed through sculptures.[133] The choice to depict the Queen in this way was a deliberate one. At the time it was considered inappropriate for a woman's body to radiate authority and political power, as well as femininity and motherhood.[134] The image of an ageing Queen solved this problem. Visible lines in the aged face of Victoria are said to convey the message that her 'body is weighed down by the sacrifices of duty in exchange for the people's love.'[135]

According to Plunkett, Victoria symbolized the maternal heart of the British Empire. The construction of the gigantic Victoria Memorial located at the end of the Mall in London supported the reshaping of London as the great capital of British Empire.[136] Both in the homeland and in the colonies, British rule had acquired mythical proportions with a trans-historical identity. The sculpted – often marble – representations of the Queen tacitly but clearly emphasized the cultural and racial differences with colonized peoples. Her ubiquitous presence in the Empire was, in Said's terms, part of imposing and perpetuating 'the quotidian processes of hegemony'.[137] The message was that the imperial mother cares of all colonial peoples as her children. This patronizing image confirmed the superiority of British rule which would bring all colonized people into an all-encompassing Western civilization. The maternal reference also softened the imposition of British authority and violent colonial exploitation.[138] Interesting in this respect is how this maternal-national iconography in India endorsed a deification of the British Queen, based on a merger of the Hindu Bharat Mata – the national personification of India as a mother goddess – and 'Ma Victoria'. Yet Indian appropriations and proclamations of deference to the late Queen Victoria were

---

[132] Freedberg 2016, 71.
[133] See https://theartwanderer.co.uk/victorian-sculpture-british-empire/.   [134] Grever 2002.
[135] Hatt 2022, 8–9.   [136] Plunkett 2022, 2.   [137] Said 1994, 131.
[138] Winston 1997, 239; Grever and Waaldijk 2004, 137.

ambiguous and complex, and at times part of internal conflicts among local populations in India. At the same time, loyalty to the maternal Queen could also be a way to criticize British rule.[139]

Monuments to Queen Victoria as an expression of imperial power and benevolent imperialism were certainly not accepted by everyone. Almost from the moment of unveiling they have been defaced and damaged. For example, in 1895, Indian nationalists and anti-colonial protesters attacked Victoria's statue in Bombay (now Mumbai), installed under a Gothic canopy. They had poured tar over her effigy and draped a garland of old sandals around her neck as an insulting parody of the regalia.[140] In 1954, Victoria's marble statue in Georgetown (British Guyana), which has stood over 58 years on the grounds of the Law Courts, was dynamited in an act of anti-colonial protest. The explosion blew off the head, smashed away the left arm which carried the orb.[141] The statue was soon repaired in England and returned to Georgetown (see Figure 11). However, after independence in 1955, inhabitants called for its removal. Local authorities did not listen. Much later, the sculpture was defaced by anti-colonial activists. A more recent example occurred in 2021, when 5,000 protesters gathered around the Victoria statue in Brisbane (Australia), one of the many replicas of the original by English sculptor Thomas Brock. They splashed the statue with red paint before wrapping it in the Aboriginal flag and held up a large sign reading 'Not the Queen's Land'.[142]

Protesters and activists often target monuments of triumphant generals, political leaders, kings and queens. The monumental imagination of Queen Victoria around the world was a prime example. Yet other figures on the pedestal with supposedly little political power can also face intense criticism. Among them is a group of men who, since the nineteenth century, were considered as humble icons of mercy: Catholic missionaries working in the colonies.

White Innocence Lost: Colonial Missionary Statues

Dozens of Catholic missionary statues stand in public spaces around the world. They have a recognizable iconography. Unlike monuments that express the undeniable omnipotence of political leaders, these sculptures carry images of self-sacrifice and holiness. Sometimes the visualization also contains militancy to convert 'uncivilized people' to Christianity. A telling example in this respect is the equestrian statue of Belgian missionary and Jesuit priest Constant Lievens with a kneeling Indian man against the pedestal both in Torpa (India) and in Moorslede (Belgium), unveiled in 1929.[143]

---

[139] Plunkett 2002, 20–21. [140] Hatt 2022, 3. [141] Winston 1997, 237. [142] Hatt 2022, 2.
[143] Goddeeris 2021, 137.

Figure 11 Repaired statue to Queen Victoria without left hand which carried the orb and damaged nose. Georgetown (Guyana). Photo David Stanly. https://commons.wikimedia.org/wiki/File:Statue_of_Queen_Victoria,_Georgetown,_Guyana.jpg

Missionaries contributed to healthcare, education and scientific work; some sought to reform the exploitation of peasants by local landowners. Caring for poor and vulnerable people in the colonies was part of their religious vocation, a task much admired.[144] Although missionary activities have long been labelled as soft colonialism, recent research also shows something else. For example, in Belgian and Dutch colonies, children were sometimes cruelly separated from their parents, communities and culture by policy officials and missionaries.[145] In this way they tried to impose their moral standards. Missionaries even intervened proactively in the lives of indigenous people, often in a paternalistic way and relying on conversion motives mixed with racist ideas. This is evident from the instruction book for missionaries in

---

[144] Monteiro 2020; Goddeeris 2022. [145] Mak, Monteiro and Wesseling 2020.

African Congo (1920), written by missionary bishop Victor Roelens. In a lengthy argument on the psychology of black people, he delivered racial judgments on their supposed laziness, selfishness, vanity, kleptomania, and lack of reasoning ability.[146] Overall, missionaries agreed with the idea of a civilizing mission, based on a Western conception of progress and white superiority. Hence the statues of missionaries standing on a pedestal, surrounded by native people kneeling or looking up. Considered as educators of white civilization, the missionaries depicted always wear a habit, while the others are (half-)naked. With increasing secularization since the 1980s, these condescending statues have provoked great anger among groups of people in former colonizing countries.

In the Netherlands, the statue of missionary Peerke Donders (1809–1887) in Tilburg is currently quite controversial.[147] Donders, born in 1809 in a village nearby, worked for many years in the Dutch colony of Suriname when slavery still existed. He nursed infected and other sick enslaved people. The statue, erected in 1926, is a national monument and property of the municipality. It shows the missionary full-length, holding a crucifix in his raised right hand; his left hand rests on the head of a kneeling man with bandaged hands (see Figure 12). While we know nothing about the kneeling man, only that he was probably African-Surinamese, the missionary was popular with Tilburg residents. Donders became a national well-known figure when the Pope beatified the missionary in 1982. At the time, the statue was occasionally defaced with mocking slogans. That was all. This benevolent attitude changed drastically in 2018, when a regional newspaper, probably inspired by Black-Lives-Matter, published a sharp protest. The newspaper received thousands of outraged responses from citizens to this attack on the statue, followed by comments on social media and heated debates in a divided city council.[148] Protests were also visible around the statue (see Figure 13).

The statue is a fascinating example of visual language that gives rise to opposing, partly overlapping interpretations. Upon closer inspection, a few things stand out. The first is the difference in posture: the white missionary stands upright with a crucifix in his raised right hand, looking down at the black kneeling man as he places his left hand on his head; the African Surinamese man looks up at the crucifix. This body language refers to a European Christian context, in which the raised crucifix can be interpreted as the triumphant display of the Catholic faith and the kneeling posture as a sign of humility and submission.[149] While kneeling in the (post)colonial context is usually regarded as a strong symbol of enslavement, in the Scriptures it means worship or

---

[146] Goddeeris 2021, 121–122. [147] Parts of this section are based on Grever 2023.
[148] Robben 2020. [149] Olko 2014, 162.

Figure 12 Statue of missionary Peerke Donders with kneeling black man. Tilburg (Netherlands). Photo John Scholte. https://nl.wikipedia.org/wiki/Standbeeld_Petrus_Donders#/media/Bestand:Tilburg_-_Wilhelminapark_Tilburg_Monument_%22Peerke_Donders%22.jpg

supplication – albeit in different situations. The standing missionary symbolizes his mediation between God and the world of people; the kneeling worshipper signifies the acknowledgement that God is greater than he is.

The laying on of the hand is an important gesture in many religions. In the Catholic faith, this is practiced by a priest at baptism and other rites of passage involving the transmission of the Holy Spirit. This also applies to white people. But the combination of the raised crucifix by missionary Donders and the laying of his hand on the head of a kneeling black Surinamese reveals that this is the conversion of a non-Christian enslaved man to the Catholic faith. From this perspective the gesture represents a superior position of the priest as mediator between God and the humble convert. Yet the gesture can also symbolize healing, such as 'praying with and for the sick, confession and forgiveness,

Figure 13 Statue of missionary Peerke Donders with BLM protest board, Tilburg (Netherlands) 2021. Photo Kenneth Cuvalay.

Source: Foto-beeld-Petrus-Donders-met-naamloze-Afrikaanse-man-Wilhelminapark-Tilburg-met-protestbord-foto-rechtenvrij.jpg

the laying on of hands, anointing with oil, and the use of charismatic spiritual gifts'.[150] The statue thus seems to refer to Donders' capability to support the healing of leprosy. Moreover, it is also a sign of his courage to touch "lepers".

Another striking element of the statue is the contrast between the bare chest of the kneeling man versus the full-dressed missionary. The asymmetrical balance of power in colonialism is reflected in the established trope of nakedness. Historian Philippa Levine explains that the unclothed African, Australian Aboriginal or Pacific Islander indicated in Victorian times an absence of civilization. She argues that colonialism's longstanding and 'seemingly timeless fascination with colonial nakedness, a perceived lack of clothing among colonized individuals' indicated 'primitiveness and savagery at least since the

---

[150] Grever 2023, 1009.

seventeenth century.'¹⁵¹ However, she also warns that neither nakedness nor nudity are fixed or universal terms or states. The attributed meanings depend on time, space, and specific cultural contexts. Whereas 'nudity' was associated with refined aesthetic representations in art and performance, especially in the colonial context 'nakedness' represented savagery and raw sexuality. Missionaries considered the unclothed body a 'profound spiritual hazard'.¹⁵² The drawings and photographs they made of colonized people supposed to demonstrate the progress of their civilizing work. This would show that conversion to Christianity had turned the 'half-naked savages' into pastoral and hard-working peasants.

Nevertheless, various Surinamese Dutch appreciate Donders for his tireless help to enslaved people and lepers. His physical touch of sick and contagious people suggested some reciprocity and respect for them at the time. In 2016, Surinamese-Dutch anthropologist Gloria Wekker – author of the book *White Innocence* – delivered the annual Peerke Donders lecture. She told the public that her late father had admired Donders.¹⁵³ He attended the beatification in Rome and always carried a small folded envelope with a fragment of Peerke's coffin in his wallet. Wekker explained that the missionary was against slavery, as he wrote in his letters home, but he had a great aversion to the religion of the Maroons, the descendants of escaped enslaved people in the rainforest. He regarded the Winti rituals as idolatry. If Donders discovered the ritual attributes during his visits, he destroyed them. Still, he was unable to Christianize them.¹⁵⁴ Wekker found the statue paternalistic and colonial.¹⁵⁵

Protests and outbursts of anger also arose at other statues of missionaries. In 2020, for instance, the statue of the Spanish missionary Junípero Serra – founder of the Indian mission in California – in Palma de Mallorca was defaced with red paint and the word 'racist' (see Figure 14).¹⁵⁶

There are many more missionary statues in other countries with similar composition and pose.¹⁵⁷ It is clear that these statues have – in the words of Wekker – lost their white innocence. Everything indicates that they belong to a genre of their own (see Figure 15). The visual language stems from older, derogatory images, such as the iconography of Christian abolitionists at the end of the eighteenth century: 'The image of kneeling blacks with folded hands, as in an attitude of prayer, the eyes turned to heaven.'¹⁵⁸ The message was also that

---

¹⁵¹ Levine 2008, 189–190.   ¹⁵² Levine 2008, 191.   ¹⁵³ Grever 2023, 1012.
¹⁵⁴ Dankelman 1982, 164–165.
¹⁵⁵ See www.wereldpodium.nu/programmas-en-activiteiten/peerke-donderslezing/peerke-donderslezing-2016-door-gloria-wekker/peerke-donderslezing-2016-lezing/.
¹⁵⁶ Grever 2023, 1010.   ¹⁵⁷ E.g. Goddeeris 2021, 138–145.
¹⁵⁸ Nederveen Pieterse 1990, 52–62.

Figure 14 Defaced statue of Spanish missionary Junipero Serra with native boy. Palma de Mallorca (Spain) 2020. Photo Jaime Reina.

abolition of slavery is an admirable goal, but only on the condition of conversion to Christianity. The Emancipation Memorial in Lincoln Park Washington D.C., erected in 1876, is a classic example of perpetuating this patronizing view of African Americans, at the same time ignoring their agency and their struggle for freedom. Abraham Lincoln is depicted with a copy of the Emancipation Proclamation in his right hand while the other hand hovers over a shirtless African American man, symbolizing the 'liberation' of enslaved people. Similar to the statue of Peerke Donders with the black man kneeling at his feet, the formerly enslaved man is depicted on one knee at Lincoln's feet. He is about to stand up, looking at the Proclamation, with one fist clenched and broken shackles at the president's feet on the pedestal. In 2020, protesters for and against the memorial demonstrated in the Lincoln Park. So far the monument has not been removed. In Boston, however, after many protests, two public

Figure 15 Statue of missionary Damiaan with leper. Leuven (Belgium). Photo Sally V. https://commons.wikimedia.org/wiki/File: Leuven_Standbeeld_Pater_Damiaan.jpg

hearings and a petition by artist Thomas Bullock signed by 12,000 people, the city decided to remove the bronze replica of the Emancipation memorial into temporary storage.[159]

'Spaces Past': Location and Relocation

Although collective memory is generally understood as a community's organized recollection of times past, it is no less connected to 'spaces past': the imaginary landscape that visualizes historical events.[160] This imaginative and

---

[159] Fazio 2020.   [160] Johnson 2005, 170.

material geography consists of different – sacred, spiritual or emotional – spaces of remembrance that can be contested and transformed over time. The exact location of memorials in a memory landscape is often of great importance. This is particularly true of the stumbling stones in memory of the victims of Nazi extermination, which are placed in the pavement in front of the victims' last home address.

Stumbling stones (German *Stolpersteine*) are small cubes with a brass plaque bearing the names and life dates of murdered Jews, Roma, Sinti, communists, Jehovah's Witnesses, and homosexuals. The laying of the stones, initiated in 1992 by German artist Gunter Demnig, aims to commemorate individuals at the *exact* last place where they lived before falling victim to Nazi persecution and terror. The project is based on research carried out by a community, family, or school. A permit for the installation of stumbling stones must be applied for with the mayor or city council. After installation, the stones become part of the sidewalk, entering public space and thus becoming the property of the municipality.[161] Each stumbling stone mentions the name of one person, with the text 'Here lived ... ' (see Figure 16). Because sometimes there is only information about where someone went to school or worked, some stones begin with 'Here studied ... ' or 'Here worked ... '.[162] Demnig places as many of the stones as possible himself. By June 2023, about 100,000 stumbling stones had been laid across Europe, including Germany, Austria, the Netherlands, Hungary, Belgium, Poland, Ukraine, Norway, and Italy.[163]

Usually, residents are informed about the placement and can file an objection. Sometimes a stone is placed a little further away from a house. This happened after consultation in Amsterdam when a female Auschwitz survivor 'could not bring herself to step over a stumbling stone that said Auschwitz every day'. In two other cases in 2017, the decision was different. After a storm of indignation, the residents of a house in Amsterdam-Zuid stopped the procedure to have a stumbling stone in front of their house removed. Later they explained to the press that they had lost a child. The stone made the processing of their loss even harder. Next, a hotel in Amsterdam did not want a stumbling stone to be placed in front of the entrance because it would not be 'cosy' for tourists. This time the objection was overruled and the stone was placed on the spot from which the Jewish people were taken to be later murdered in a concentration camp.[164] This last example shows that even though a stumbling stone is small, it can apparently still disturb people or make them think about the message it contains. That is precisely the intention of the sculptor. One cannot simply ignore them. They

---

[161] See www.stolpersteine.eu/en/the-art-memorial/schritte-zur-stolperstein-verlegung.
[162] See www.stolpersteine.eu/en/. [163] Cook and Van Riemsdijk 2014.
[164] Kruyswijk 2017; KNAW 2023, 62.

Figure 16 Stumbling stones. Amsterdam (Netherlands) 2018. Photo Photojack50. https://nl.wikipedia.org/wiki/Bestand: Stolpersteine_for_the_Pollack_family,_Amsterdam_October_3,_2018.jpg

are a personalized reminder of the horrors of the Shoah. This modest representation without any decoration or symbols has a powerful effect. The message is: *here*, in this house, people lived or worked; they were taken away and murdered; do not forget them. In this case location is compelling.

After a change of political regime, the location of a monument in a memory landscape can very sensitive. This was evident in the commotion surrounding the so-called Bronze Soldier in Tallinn, the capital of Estonia. To understand this, one must consider the recent political history of this Baltic country. Although it had declared neutrality at the outbreak of the Second World War, the Soviet Union (USSR) invaded Estonia in 1940, followed a year later by Germany; the country was reoccupied by the USSR in 1944. During the war years (1941–1944), Estonian military units fought with the Germans, seen as 'liberators', against the Soviets. On 18 September, 1944, the Germans retreated and an Estonian shadow government was formed. Four days later the Red Army occupied Tallinn, and from 1944 to 1991 Estonia was an administrative Soviet state. After the bloodless 'Singing revolution' against USSR rule, Estonia regained its independence as a sovereign democratic republic on 20 August, 1991. Nowadays, the country has 1.4 million inhabitants, including a large Russian minority (23,7%); in Tallinn, about 47% of the capital are non-Estonians, mostly Russians.

The Bronze Soldier, unveiled in 1947, was a 'Monument to the Liberators of Tallinn' commemorating the Soviet victory over the Nazis. The two-metre bronze statue of a Red Army soldier on a stonewall structure above a burial site of Soviet soldiers' remains was located in a park in central Tallinn (see Figure 17). After Estonian independence in 1991 it was re-named 'Monument to the Fallen of the Second World War', by way of adjusting the Soviet narrative

Figure 17 The 'Bronze Soldier' monument after relocation. Tallinn (Estonia), 27 September 2007. Photo Karsten Brüggemann.

of 'liberating' Estonia.[165] Nevertheless, for the time being the monument remained in the same location, surviving the wave of purging Soviet symbols and monuments as a response to the long-lasting presence of Soviet iconography. However, public monuments that fail to recognize a new political power or movement will ultimately draw attention to the one-sided state of the existing mnemonic landscape. This happened also to the Bronze Soldier in Tallinn.

Marek Tamm has described how in the 1990s, a new memory politics emerged to construct historical continuity based on a desire to return to pre-war traditions, 'to restore everything destroyed or condemned to neglect by the Soviet period'.[166] The new memory politics included the restoration of monuments to the War of Independence, the renaming of streets and houses, and the erection of new memorials. In 2002, a new memorial to commemorate Estonian soldiers who fought alongside the Germany army in the Second World War was unveiled in Pärnu, to be removed nine days later. The bronze bas-relief represented an Estonian soldier with Nazi military symbols on his uniform.[167] Two years later, on the initiative of a local council, the same monument was re-erected in Lihula. Estonian veterans and neo-Nazi's attended the unveiling ceremony, which was widely criticized in the country and abroad. Under this pressure, the government removed the monument again and supported its location in the private Museum of the Struggle for Estonia's Freedom.

This raised questions in the newspapers and other media as to why a monument to Estonian soldiers in German uniforms should be removed, while monuments to the Soviet army, such as the Bronze Soldier in Tallinn, were still standing. Increasingly, calls were made to move the entire Soviet monument. Soon after, in 2005, the monument was defaced with red paint, followed by discussions in Parliament, demonstrations, TV interviews, cyber attacks conducted by Russia, and direct clashes between opponents and supporters of the monument. A group of Russian Estonians formed a Night Watch to protect the monument from damage or displacement. In 2007, after many more protests, the government relocated the Bronze Soldier to the Cemetery of Estonian Defence Forces, the public military cemetery where 5,000 soldiers are buried, including 550 who died in the Estonian war of Independence.[168] The monument remains there intact, viewable by the public.

The monument crisis in Estonia in 2007 illustrated the diverse war experiences and conflicting interpretations of the inhabitants, resulting in a cooled relationship with Russia and increasing international tensions. However, the point was also that the (re)location of the War Memorial in Pärnu and the Bronze

---

[165] Ryback, Ellis and Glahn eds. 2021, 148.   [166] Tamm 2013, 654.   [167] Idem, 666.
[168] Ryback, Ellis and Glahn eds. 2021, 157–158.

Soldier in Tallinn revealed the dominance of Soviet narratives in the memory landscape at that time. The protests thus primarily aimed at a change of the 'spaces past': a transformation of the visualized Estonian mnemonic regime.

Aniconic Monuments of Trauma

As discussed in Section 3, in the interwar-period, there was a gradual shift in memorial design. The change was accompanied by a transition from nationalistic veneration of canonized 'heroes' on high pedestals to commemoration and recognition of common soldiers and civilian victims symbolized by the Unknown Soldier and the Mourning Mother. The vertical style of the triumphant statues required visitors to literally look up at the represented figures. In the last quarter of the twentieth century, due to the experiences of the Second World War and the Holocaust, artists created abstract, aniconic monuments – often engraved with names of the many dead – that try to do justice to the incomprehensible, deliberate destruction of masses of people. The horizontal shape and style of these memorials place greater emphasis on mourning the victims and remembering the loss, compared to the heroic and often intimidating vertical statues. Another trend that emerged were so-called counter-monuments: confrontational constellations that criticize the monumental qualities of traditional statues. In Section 5, I will delve deeper into this phenomenon.

The Vietnam Veterans Memorial in Washington D.C. (1982) was one of the first horizontal abstract monuments. The memorial consists of a bronze group of three soldiers in combat gear by Frederick Hart and two large polished granite walls with the names of service members who died or remain missing during the war (see Figure 18). The walls, designed by American architect Maya Lin, initially caused a lot of controversy. Lin introduced a new architectural language, a minimalist style that does not glorify war.[169] The walls give visitors little information, but rather allow them to reflect on the history to which they refer. Other examples include the Nagasaki National Peace Memorial Hall for the Atomic Bomb Victims (2002) and the Memorial to the Murdered Jews of Europe in Berlin (2004).

Visitors must give meaning to the monument themselves, since it does not provide the closure of a heroic history like the heroic statues. In addition, Wagoner and Bresco, and other scholars point to the possible healing function of these monuments that aim to transform painful and traumatic experiences of the descendants of victims. Such monuments reduce the distance to visitors, encouraging them to reflect on the past and to process both individual and collective wounds, inviting multi-sensory exploration and more interaction.[170]

---

[169] Wolfson 2017.
[170] Wagoner and Bresco 2022, 1–2, 17; Watkins, Cole and Weidemann 2010.

Figure 18 Wall of Vietnam Veterans Memorial. Washington D.C. (USA). Photo National Park Service. https://en.wikipedia.org/wiki/ Vietnam_Veterans_Memorial#/media/File: Vietnam_Veterans_Memorial_reflection_in_low_light.jpg

This shift is most noticeable at the Holocaust Memorial in Berlin, designed by Peter Eisenman, which consists of 2,711 blocks or 'stelae', arranged in a grid pattern on a sloping field. This creates long, straight, narrow alleys between the blocks, along which the ground undulates. An adjoining, secured underground information space contains the names of some 3 million Jewish Holocaust victims, obtained from the Israeli museum Yad Vashem. Visitors may feel uneasy and disoriented as they walk through the narrow alleys along the tall blocks, which is exactly what Eisenman had in mind. He intended for visitors to get a sense of the immense displacement and destruction of those millions of people. The erection of the Holocaust Monument also marked the end of the so-called communicative phase in the culture of remembrance of the Shoah, in which the last survivors and their (grand)children can testify about camp experiences.[171] What remains is the cultural phase of collective memory, such as archiving, publications, heritage and monuments, the indirect and constructed memories. Public monuments and statues as expressions of cultural memory that commemorate genocide or other traumas are incredibly important. They are a foothold for the descendants, the recognition of their ancestors'

---

[171] Assmann 2008.

suffering. In addition, they offer an opportunity to acquire knowledge about the past and perhaps more understanding of people's behaviour. In this way it also supports historical consciousness.

The National Holocaust Names Monument in Amsterdam, recently unveiled in 2021, fits into the international trend of aniconic representations and the listing of names of victims – more than 122,000 Jewish victims, Sinti and Roma from the Netherlands – whose remains are no longer present at a particular location.[172] The current naming of victims comes from the tradition at the war cemeteries and memorials erected since the nineteenth century. But the Vietnam Veterans Memorial gave a new impetus to this tradition, enabling individuals to make meaning of the disaster and to personally connect with the collective past.[173] Without these names, the scale of a catastrophe is difficult to grasp, reduced to only an abstract number. Other well-known examples of these public monuments are the Wall of Remembrance in Buenos Aires with the names of thousands of people who went missing during the Videla regime, the Kigali Memorial Monument in Rwanda with the names of victims of the genocide against the Tutsis, and the recently unveiled Memorial to the Abolition of Slavery in Nantes.

In 1994, on the occasion of the commemoration of the Holocaust, Andreas Huyssen stressed the urgency of a tangible materialized memorial with a public and dialogical dimension because millions had been murdered anonymously. The dehumanization of camp prisoners, the horror and the scale of this genocide cannot possibly literary depicted. Huyssen therefore advocated a multi-interpretable and abstract type of monument that stimulates dialogue among visitors.[174]

5 Dialogical Monuments in a Global Media Network

In Ukraine today, statues and monuments of Russian poet Alexander Pushkin are absent from public spaces, either removed or covered with spray-painted graffiti, and awaiting destruction from Russian bombardments without protective sandbags. In 2015, after Russia's invasion of Crimea, the Ukrainian government signed a new decolonization law, which echoes the earlier removal of Lenin and Marx statues and the renaming of communist street names. In this case, the legislation targets monuments embodying Russian imperialism, whether during the Tsarist Russian Empire or the Soviet era, including literary figures such as Pushkin.[175]

So, depending on prior knowledge and the circumstances of the moment, people view, and interpret monuments in manifold ways. Although this can lead to conflicts, the result is that divergent cultural interpretations keep the past

---

[172] KNAW 2023, 124–127.   [173] Wagoner and Bresco 2022, 16.   [174] Huyssen 1994, 16.
[175] Plokhy 2023.

alive. Equally important is to realize that seemingly unchanging monuments in public space are nodes of a cultural memory in a dynamic global media network. The role of traditional media was evident in the case of the protests against missionary statues and the monument crisis in Estonia in 2007 (see Section 4). But the rise of new (social) media has further strengthened the intertwining of tangible representations and their visualization in the media. Today, (moving) images of monuments and statues, including actions for and against them, circulate rapidly from one medium to another around the world through newspapers, television, online exhibitions, Instagram, LinkedIn, and other social media. The impact of multi-media was especially noticeable during the Rhodes Must Fall movement of 2015. The campaign for the removal of the statue of Cecil Rhodes – Prime Minister of the Cape Colony (1890–1896) – at the University of Cape Town received global attention and quickly led to a wider movement to 'decolonise' education across South-Africa and other countries around the world. So, monuments 'never stand alone'.[176] Embedded both in tangible memory landscapes and global multimedia networks they are actors in these 'shifting assemblages that bring together material objects, narratives, locations, and human actors in changing constellations',[177] influencing the memory landscape and vice versa.

This section explores these shifting assemblages. Through interactions in the media and public interventions, landscapes of memory are being transformed worldwide. Sometimes the process of mnemonic change goes hand in hand with a growing awareness of its deeply gendered character.

Public Monumental Interventions

After a regime change, a government can decide to dismantle or relocate a monument. As described above, such intervention in the memory landscape happened in the context of the de-Sovietization of Ukraine. Another example of deliberate disappearance are Confederate statues and monuments across the US. After years of campaigning, arguing that their presence still justified racism, they were removed by order of state or city governments. Yet in 2025, president Trump ordered another public intervention: the creation of a National Garden of American Heroes featuring 250 life-size statues, including those of Confederate generals.[178] To accommodate protests, a government or other official body may also choose to adapt the memory landscape by having so-called compensation monuments or counter-monuments erected. Interventions in a landscape of memory also occur when activists modify monuments with graffiti, deform or

---

[176] Rigney 2022, 14.   [177] Grever 2025A.
[178] See www.mensjournal.com/news/trump-administration-national-park-american-heroes.

tear them down with ropes, and throw them into the water, as the crowd in Bristol in 2020 did to the statue of slave-trader Edward Colston. The remains – pieces of a statue or an empty plinth – are then used to build innovative public constructions.

The activist modification strategy is particularly interesting because it means that not all monuments during iconoclast conflicts disappear completely. Some are transformed into so-called 'anti-monuments': ephemeral – often creative – structures of local collective memory, rooted in contestation. They can turn cities into 'the stage on which public spaces are claimed and reclaimed with political purposes'.[179] Anti-monuments are a popular phenomenon in Latin America, especially in Mexico. They collectively refer to massacres, forced disappearances, and violence against women.[180] According to Lorena Solano, anti-monuments are living symbols of resistance and the performance of public memory and mourning. She describes how Colombia's 2021 social uprising against higher taxes, corruption and health reforms proposed by the government of President Iván Duque, saw tens of thousands of people take to the streets. Despite peaceful demonstrations, protesters clashed with police who used brutal force. At least five people died and more than 1,100 people were injured. Cali, the capital of the Department of Valle del Cauca in the southwest of Colombia, in particular, was the epicentre of the protests and a symbol of resistance to state violence. During over three months of large-scale protests, the city became an iconic site of resistance that redefined public space.[181]

One large monument symbolizes this development: La Mano (the Hand) or the Monument to Resistance. La Mano is a large and colourful sculpture of a raised left fist 9,50 metres high, located in Puerto Rellena southeast of Cali (see Figure 19). It represents the hand of Kay Kimi Krachi, the Mayan god of battle, and was built during the protests against the statue of Sebastián de Belalcazar, the Spanish founder of early colonial cities in Colombia. On 28 April, 2021, members of the indigenous Misak community overthrew Belalcazar.[182] The Hand holds a sign with the word 'Resist' and is adorned with the names and faces of several of the people who died in the framework of the massive protests and all the widespread social unrest that hit Colombia between April and July 2021.[183]

After an appeal, the community of Cali donated the necessary materials for the construction, which was carried out in two weeks. Its inauguration on 13 June was attended by thousands of people. However, rumours circulated about the government's intention to dismantle La Mano. Citizens collected

---

[179] Villamil-Valencia 2024.   [180] Díaz-Tovar 2018; Gutiérrez 2024.   [181] Solano 2024, 2.
[182] See www.apollo-magazine.com/colombia-statues-conquistadores-toppling/.
[183] Solano 2024, 7–8.

Figure 19 La Mano, Monument of Resistance. Cali (Colombia). Photo Remux. https://es.wikipedia.org/wiki/Monumento_a_la_Resistencia

signatures to request the mayor of Cali not to do so. Finally, on 24 March, 2022, the mayor confirmed that the 'monument to the resistance will not be demolished'.[184] He recognized that the sculpture, in memory of the victims during the social uprising, has become an important social symbol. According to the city council, it will remain in the square of 'Puerto Resistancia'.

Whereas anti-monuments are a response to social and political developments in society, counter-monuments and compensation monuments emphasize something else. The conceptual difference between the concepts is subtle, sometimes fuzzy and subject to discussion.[185] Generally, counter-monuments not only

---

[184] See www.infobae.com/en/2022/03/24/this-would-cost-america-from-cali-to-get-juan-carlos-osorio-out-2/.
[185] Young 1992; Van Houwelingen 2020.

criticize hegemonic ideologies about inequality and superiority, but also the idea of a homogeneous past represented by a mimetic physical construction. They show a new paradigm of a memory landscape by questioning the assumed property of a monument as a fixed anchor point of time and meaning. Unlike the self-aggrandizing male heroes on high pedestals, counter-monuments are often confrontational and alienating. They fit into the aniconic trend discussed in the previous section. According to one expert in memory studies and Holocaust memorials, they provoke reflection and discomfort, highlighting silenced voices and focusing on what is forgotten or omitted.[186] In Germany, for example, conceptual artists Jochen Gerz and Esther Shalev-Gerz constructed in 1986 a 'Monument against Fascism' in Hamburg. It was a twelve-meter-high, one square pillar covered with lead, which slowly sank into the ground until it disappeared. The whole construction symbolized a critique of fascism, but above all it meant a *deconstruction* of its own existence: it desecrated itself and rebelled against the cherished conventions of monuments that want to preserve memory and time forever. Passers-by were invited to write their names and comments in the soft lead on the sinking pillar. By 1993, the monument was completely sunk into the ground, as was the graffiti of the public.[187] The whole process was an indictment of the sanctification of traditional heroic monuments and an invitation to the public to reflect and enter into dialogue with one another. What remains is the memory of the disappeared monumental pillar and the dialogues held about its meaning.

Like counter-monuments, compensation monuments demonstrate the exclusive and one-sided character of a memory landscape. In this context, compensation means that there is a qualitative deficit, a lack or loss of who and what is or is not represented that needs to be remedied and corrected.[188] Contested monuments and statues are not removed or destroyed but 'compensated' by new and corrective structures. These physical constructions and sites literary aim to compensate for the monumental imbalance in a landscape of memory and are often created after a regime change.

In South Africa, for example, in 1994, after the abolition of apartheid and the installation of Nelson Mandela's Government of National Unity, efforts were made to reshape the memory landscape in an attempt to break the dominance of apartheid representations and create a new, inclusive identity for the nation.[189] Research in the 1990s had indicated that almost all public monuments reflected the history and values of the previous white regime.[190] The ANC government, various organizations, and individuals started to commission statues and

---

[186] Young 1992, 273–274; Solano 2024, 4.   [187] Seligmann-Silva 2020, 155.
[188] Kouzelis, Rönn and Teräväinen eds. 2022, 7–8.   [189] Vosloo and Young 2020.
[190] Schönfeldt-Aultman 2006, 217–218.

monuments dedicated to black resistance fighters and groundbreaking events against the apartheid regime. An impressive project in this regard is the state-funded Freedom Park, built on Salvokop Hill overlooking Pretoria.[191] Inspired by an idea from then-President Mandela, it was soon conceived as a monumental plan to symbolise a reconciled nation and correct the one-sided memory landscape.[192] The Park – opened in 2004 and set on a 52-hectare site – was designed by landscape architects who were tasked with creating a meaningful commemorative place for the South African people.[193] The new leaders had envisioned a memorial site, where, as Mandela had described, 'we shall honour with all the dignity they deserve, those who endured pain so we can experience the joy of freedom.'[194] The eventually completed Freedom Park – in effect one large compensation monument – pursues this goal. Particularly striking is the Isivivane memorial, part of the Park museum and commemorative complex (see Figure 20). It is situated in a location overlooking the surrounding area, echoing the Voortrekker Monument on another high point

Figure 20 Isivivane – Freedom Park. Pretoria (South Africa). Photo Shosholoza. https://upload.wikimedia.org/wikipedia/commons/8/8c/Isivivani.jpg

---

[191] Labuschagne 2010, 115.
[192] Vosloo and Young 2020, 87. See also www.freedompark.co.za/.
[193] Labuschagne 2010, 112.
[194] See https://nathankrees.com/freedom-park-and-the-voortrekker-monument/.

in the vicinity. It consists of ten rocks, each from the different provinces of South Africa, symbolizing unity.

The Freedom Park is within direct view of the immense Voortrekker Monument, which honours the Boers' Great Trek and the Battle of Blood River in 1838. This had given conservative white Afrikaners a sense of pride in their heritage. Although the Zulu had suffered mostly from the Great Trek and the Battle of the Blood River, it was decided not to destroy the monument – if that were even possible given its gigantic size – but to create the Freedom Park as an alternative vision of South Africa. The Park includes a museum and up the hillside a series of memorial spaces, like the 'Wall of Names', listing South Africans killed in conflict and wars, including both world wars. The Voortrekker Monument is a classically inspired emblem of Western monumentality in the service of colonialism with a clearly defined narrative. Freedom Park offers an open-ended contemplation and stimulates a critical dialogue with (and against) the Voortrekker Monument.[195]

According to Labuschange and others, the site generated a fair amount of negative response. For example, the placement of the Park opposite the Voortrekker Monument did not really support the ideal of peace and reconciliation. The criticism is that mainly current political reasons determined the choice of location and design, while a historicizing approach that establishes a connection with original inhabitants and ancestors is missing: 'the atmosphere and the spirituality that the park wishes to portray is an *invented history*'.[196] Nevertheless, recent research into the park's reception among visitors shows that the site is meaningful for many South Africans. People experience it as an important site of memory, a safe place for reflection, healing, and beauty.[197]

While compensation monuments aim to supplement or correct the monumental imbalance of a memory landscape, other physical public representations are a constant critical thorn in the side of institutions or governments. They are silent provocative protests. Famous in this respect are the hidden mini-statues of Ukrainian-Hungarian artist Mihály Kolodko, such as a murdered squirrel, a tiny tank, or a Hungarian doll, that pop up in unexpected corners on streets, window ledges and bridges of Budapest.[198] Kolodko's first mini-statue was Mr. Worm, the main character from a Hungarian children's TV-series (see Figure 21).

Kolodko, living in Budapest since 2016, is a kind of guerrilla sculptor who has created at least 30 mini-statues in the city, inviting passers-by to discover them. They are melded in the city landscape and show again that size does not matter but art does. The statuettes – figures from well-known American and

---

[195] See www.sawarmemorials.ed.ac.uk/.   [196] Labuschagne 2010, 117–118.
[197] Vosloo and Young 2020, 113–114.
[198] See https://budapestflow.com/hidden-mini-statues-budapest/ and www.modernhobos.com/stories/travel-essays/the-guerilla-sculptures-of-budapest/.

Figure 21 Statuette Mr Worm by Mykhailo Kolodko. Budapest (Hungary). Photo Elekes Andor. https://commons.wikimedia.org/wiki/File:F%C5% 91kukac_(2).jpg

lesser-known Hungarian cartoons – are anthropomorphic animals performing human activities. One of Kolodko's statues is clearly political: the 2022 bronze mini-figure of Russian President Vladimir Putin in a warship, placed on a column in the shape of a middle finger. The construction refers to the famous phrase of the Ukrainian border guard on Snake Island to the Russian missile cruiser 'Moskva' in February 2022: 'Russian warship, go fuck yourself'.[199] Nevertheless, although the mini-statues are a subtle protest against Hungarian MPs' or the government's decisions, most of the installations are funny, sweet and very popular among the citizens of Budapest. This is completely different from the provocative, life-size statues of so-called 'comfort women', which call for recognition and justice.

'Comfort Women' Memorials: Tangible Symbols of Peace

Between 1932 and 1945, the Imperial Japanese Army had forced women from occupied Asian countries to become so-called 'comfort women', a euphemism for sex slaves used by the Japanese military. The United Nations estimates that this numbered around 200,000 women,[200] some as young as thirteen, who were tricked into false jobs or kidnapped and coerced into sexual slavery in so-called 'comfort stations', brothels run by the

---

[199] Eröss 2022, 81–83.
[200] Ling 2009, 63; Shim 2023, 665. Other researchers estimate that around 400,000 women and girls were involved. See Aquino and Martin 2023, 261.

Imperial Army. Japanese women were not recruited. The brothels provided a stable 'pool of prostitutes' that would 'satisfy' the sexual desires of Japanese soldiers. In this way, sexually transmitted diseases could also be better controlled, reduced and prevented. The system resulted in women suffering constant extreme physical and psychological harm, often ending in death at the time or later. There are testimonies of women being raped twenty to thirty times every night for seven years.[201] It took years before the victims dared to tell about their horrific experiences. Due to existing taboos and shame about their past, they were forced to remain silent by their families and communities. Moreover, the women were often not listened to.[202]

When the first allegations from victims surfaced in 1991, Japanese politicians denied any responsibility and referred to private contractors who had organized the brothels. Two years later, after publications with evidence of the crimes, things turned around. During state visits to South Korea, Japanese ministers apologized. Of great significance was the Kono Statement by the progressive Japanese government in 1993, which acknowledged that its 'administrative / military personnel directly took part' in the forced recruitment of women to the 'comfort stations'.[203] However, some conservative historians stated that the women voluntarily joined the stations. In 1995, the Liberalist History Research group opposed against the government's decision to include lines about 'comfort women' in textbooks.[204] Subsequently, in 2000, the newly established Japanese Society for History Textbook Reform published the *New History Textbook,* which presented a revised view of Japanese history. The aim was to 'correct history' and offer a more positive view of Japan's past by removing references to atrocities such as medical experiments on prisoners and 'comfort women'.[205] Many historians and educators protested the whitewashing of Japan's wartime activities, but conservative governments adopted this line of thinking. In 2007, then Prime Minister Shinzō Abe, leader of the Liberal Democratic Party, claimed that there was no evidence of coercion, sparking international outrage, particularly from South Korea and the US. The issue of 'wartime sex slaves' was soon removed from most authorized high school history textbooks. Today, this history remains controversial. Only one of twelve high school textbooks mentions the coercive nature of the Japanese military system of sexual slavery.[206]

Nevertheless, since 1992, every Wednesday there have been demonstrations for the recognition of the victims of forced prostitution outside the Japanese

---
[201] Tongsuthi 1994, 415. [202] Ling 2009, 69; Janssen 2010; Banning 2012.
[203] Chapman 2021, 425. [204] Ryback, Ellis and Glahn eds. 2021, 179.
[205] Woods Masalski 2001.
[206] See www.voanews.com/a/fact-check-comfort-women-japan-textbooks/6743139.html.

embassy in Seoul (South Korea), initiated by The Korean Council for the Women Drafted for Military Sexual Slavery. Survivors and supporters demanded justice, an official apology from the Japanese government and a memorial for the survivors in the form of a column. However, South Korean sculptors Kim Seo-kyung and Kim Eun-sung decided not to design an abstract column but a recognizable statue. On December 14, 2011, at the occasion of the 1000th Wednesday demonstration by the Council, 'The Statue of a Girl for Peace' was installed in front of the Japanese embassy to keep a permanent vigil. The life-size bronze statue shows a young girl sitting barefoot in a chair, staring straight ahead, her fists clenched in her lap. She has short-cropped hair and is wearing a *hanbok*, a traditional Korean dress. On her left shoulder sits a small bird, symbolizing freedom and peace. Next to her is an empty chair, a memorial to the many 'comfort women' who died and were unable to fight for justice (see Figure 22). It is also a symbolic invitation to young generations to support women's struggle against sexual violence.[207]

Figure 22 'Comfort woman' statue in front of the Japanese Embassy. Seoul (South Korea). Photo bong9@hani.co.kr. https://wiki.ubc.ca/ Mistreatment_of_Comfort_Women_Under_Imperial_Japanese_Army_Rule#/ media/File:Comfort_Women_Statue.jpg

---

[207] See www.projectsonyeo.com/statueofpeace.

The Japanese government strongly condemned the statue, demanding its removal.[208] Nevertheless, life-size copies of the statue – sometimes with modifications or extensions but always based on the original design – were rapidly distributed to other locations in South Korea and countries with Korean Diaspora communities, including the US, Australia, Canada, China, Taiwan, and Germany.[209] In this way, the statues have become part of the trans-national and global memory of the Second World War. The peace statues led to several years of diplomatic tensions between South Korea and the US on the one hand and Japan on the other.

In 2015, Japan's foreign Minister promised to provide money for a fund for surviving 'comfort women' on condition that the Peace Statue in front of the embassy in Seoul be removed. Initially, South Korean Prime Minister Park Geun-hye promised to relocate it. But this did not happen. Large-scale civil protests against this decision attracted worldwide media attention, and supporters protected the statue on a daily basis.[210] The background to the resistance was also the fear that its removal would contribute to a renewed silence about the victims and the erasure of their memories.[211] According to David Shim, the demand to remove a particular monument or statue is not new in itself, but a government's insistence on removing a memorial statue to wartime victims in a foreign country is unprecedented,[212] especially one that is a former belligerent during the Second World War, such as Japan. It demonstrates the limitations of a country to control its historical narratives beyond its territorial borders.[213] Perhaps even more striking is that despite new (social) media with information and images about the sexual exploitation of women by the former Japanese Imperial Army, a tangible mimetic statue was apparently considered a guarantee against amnesia.

Although the statue remained standing opposite the Japanese embassy, in 2015 the embassy itself was moved to the Twin Tree Tower as a temporary location while its building was being renovated. A high fence was built around the original location (see Figure 23). Due to conflicts with the Seoul city government over the renovation, the embassy is still under construction. On *Google Maps*, the fence can be seen, including photos of demonstrations. Because there are also police buses stationed in this area as security, the line of site from the statue to the location is even more blocked. Meanwhile, in Seoul, Toronto and other cities, sympathizers wrap the girl in warm clothes during winter. Often visitors empathetically touch the statue and make

---

[208] Shim 2023, 665.
[209] See www.projectsonyeo.com/statueofpeace (2024). For the US, McCarthy 2014; for Taiwan, Ward 2018.
[210] Ryback, Ellis and Glahn eds. 2021, 181–182.   [211] Shim, 2023, 668.
[212] Shim, 2023, 666–667.   [213] Ryback, Ellis and Glahn eds. 2021, 187.

Figure 23 Same 'comfort woman' statue, seen from behind, wearing a woollen cap. The entrance to the Embassy is blocked. Photo Sakaori. https://upload.wikimedia.org/wikipedia/commons/3/36/Japanese_Embassy_in_Seoul_and_watched_from_behind_a_bronze_statue_of_comfort_women.JPG

selfies.[214] A more recent, remarkable action is the placement of a copied 'comfort woman' statue on seats of buses in Seoul that pass the Japanese embassy every day, with passengers hearing audio clips of testimonies from former victims.[215] This creative protest allows a normally immobile structure to move, making it nearly impossible for downtown citizens, including staff of the Japanese embassy, to ignore.

While Shim has emphasized the power of the Statue of Peace's material rhetoric, others point to its emotional potential in giving expression to historical injustices and capturing public's attention.[216] It is clear in this case that a public statue can exert a certain power.[217] David Chapman reflects on the impact of the combination of physical reproductions and digital media, which extends its visual presence in the world and stimulates communication with people in various contexts.[218] The interaction between the physical/tangible and the online/digital around the 'Comfort Women' Memorials impressively

---

[214] See e.g. https://nowtoronto.com/news/hidden-toronto-the-comfort-woman-statue/.
[215] Shim, 2023, 667. See e.g. www.npr.org/sections/parallels/2017/11/13/563838610/comfort-woman-memorial-statues-a-thorn-in-japans-side-now-sit-on-korean-buses.
[216] Shim 2023, 672–673.   [217] Freedberg 2016, 68.   [218] Chapman 2021, 431.

demonstrates the potential performative power that monuments in public space have and their impact on negotiations of regional and international political relations.

Decolonising Gendered Landscapes of Memory

In debates about the impact of centuries of colonialism in the Western world, conflicts over public monuments play an important role in attempts to decolonise public space. This call for decolonization began with the outrage over colonial statues and other public representations in the 1960s, during the struggles for independence of colonized regions in Africa, Asia, Latin America, and the black civil rights movement in the US.[219] There was a growing awareness in these countries that modern cities were arenas for showcasing white superiority. Another, related phenomenon were the emerging protests of First Nations about the occupied lands of their ancestors in Latin America, the US, Canada, Australia, and the Middle East. Publications of postcolonial research stimulated the dissemination of historical knowledge about colonialism, orientalism, racism and whiteness.[220] Moreover, new aesthetic conceptualizations challenged the static features traditionally associated with the commemorative function of public heroic monuments. They demonstrated the bias of historical narratives and collective memory, such as the history of colonialism, slavery and the dehumanization of people.

As described earlier, relatives and descendants of enslaved black people often experience the presence of some public monuments in former colonizing empires as painful and offensive. According to Clara Gatugu, public space is still littered with numerous colonial references that illustrate the unequal and racialized relations between former colonizers and colonized individuals. Allowing these to continue to exist normalizes racism and other hierarchical relationships. Therefore, in many countries, voices have been raised to *decolonise* public spaces by moving or removing monuments that glorify political leaders from the colonial period, by creating new (compensation) monuments and renaming streets and squares.[221] However, such a change in the memory landscape must be accompanied by various activities, such as organizing dialogues between citizens, teachers, curators, local, and national authorities, setting up special memorial days and a documentation center, and transforming education. The assumption is that decolonization processes can succeed if they

---

[219] Ramirez 2024.
[220] E.g. Young 1995; Harris 1993; Frederickson 2002; Moreton-Robinson 2015.
[221] Gatugu 2022.

address 'the enduring structures of power that perpetuate colonial hierarchies and injustices at the intersections of race, class, sexuality and gender'.[222]

Anti-racist protests gained momentum in 2020, following the killing of George Floyd. Influenced by demonstrations and iconoclastic actions, widely visible on social media, various national and regional governments, associations and communities in the US, South Africa, Europe, Canada, and other former colonizing or settler powers set up committees to consider the meaning of decolonization and to reflect on a collaborative re-design of public spaces with local residents, including indigenous people.[223] It was a response to processes of forgetting and silencing the colonial past. In addition, the spatial turn in the humanities and social sciences has led to a critical evaluation of public spaces, with the concept of 'mapping' being an attempt to also emphasize space and place in understanding the past and its long-term impact effects in the present.[224]

In the Netherlands, monuments have now been erected in cities to commemorate slavery. Since 2002, the national slavery monument has been located in Amsterdam, followed by monuments in Middelburg (2005), Rotterdam (2013), Utrecht (2023), and the Hague (2025). A Dutch *Slavery Heritage Guide* provides information about material traces of the slavery past in the public sphere.[225] The Guide is the product of the Dutch Mapping Slavery project, a team of critical heritage experts who perform a kind of archaeology of the present, tracing the physical remains of slavery in the Dutch public sphere.[226] In Belgium, the numerous public representations of King Leopold II, 'owner of his private domain Congo Free State', had provoked ferocious protests. In 2022, a parliamentary 'Special Commission on the Colonial Past' published a report raising the question to what extent decolonization requires the erasure of traces that are experienced as offensive.[227] So far, there have been few concrete decolonizing interventions in the Belgian public space. Nevertheless, there is a growing awareness in countries around the world that memory landscapes are often one-sided and hardly recognizable for people living in an increasingly multicultural society. Moreover, statues have also been erected to celebrate resistance fighters against colonialism and racism: e.g. Nelson Mandela in Pretoria (2013), Anton de Kom in Amsterdam (2016), Malawi's anti-colonial hero John Chilembwe in London (2022), Algerian freedom fighter Emir Abdelkader in Amboise (2022) – damaged even before its unveiling, but restored again. Attempts in 2018, to erect a statue of the assassinated Congolese Prime Minister Patrice Lumumba in Brussels have so far failed.[228]

---

[222] Van Ruyskensvelde and Berghmans 2024, 133.   [223] Jawanda 2022.
[224] Modest 2019, VIII.
[225] Hondius, Jouwe, Stam and Tosch 2019 and www.blackheritagetours.com/.
[226] Modest 2019, VIII–IX.   [227] Colar 2023.   [228] Gatugu 2022.

Despite widespread international calls to decolonise urban spaces and public sites, the gender-specific features remain salient. Memory landscapes consist of an overwhelming number of male heroes placed on pedestals worldwide, surrounded by representations of female symbols such as 'Liberty' and 'Justice', and holy women like Mother Mary. The editors of the educational handbook *A Space of our own* even speak of 'the extreme under-representation of women in monuments'.[229] Although women have historically left their mark on socio-economic and political changes as resistance fighters, activists, workers, politicians, writers, poets, scientists, inventors, and so on, researched by numerous (feminist) historians in academic books and peer reviewed articles, monuments of them are still rare.[230] Exceptions are monuments of queens, grieving mothers, and especially female war victims, such as the statues of 'comfort women' discussed above, or the Strength and Remembrance Pole in North Vancouver (Canada) commemorating the missing and murdered indigenous women and girls.[231] The aforementioned temporary anti-monuments in Latin America are also often dedicated to femicide and violence against women.

Representations of women can also be found among the various monuments associated with historically alleged witchcraft. In early modern history several witch hunts have taken place in Europe and the Americas. Society was said to be threatened by a sect, whose members conspired with the devil to spread death and destruction. The suspects were mostly isolated adult women – midwives, widows, women with physical disabilities, healers with knowledge of medicinal plants – although the persecution could also affect men and young girls.[232] Causes related to demographic shifts from the 1450s when the European population increased explosively, while food prices rose and wages decreased.[233] In times of political unrest or disaster, vulnerable people often functioned as scapegoats. They were often tortured, hanged, or burned at the stake without trial. Most estimates put the number of executed persons at 45,000–60,000 in Europe and North America; 80–85 per cent of those sentenced were women.

Among the earliest memorials is the Witches Well Monument, unveiled in Edinburgh in 1894. It commemorates the brutal Scottish witch hunts between 1479 and 1722 with hundreds of victims. Today, the monument is criticized for implying that those executed had magical powers and were therefore not innocent.[234] In 1992, a Witch Trial Monument was unveiled in Salem

---

[229] Plümer-Bardak ed. 2023, 7.   [230] De Vries 2021, 8–10.
[231] See www.kairoscanada.org/missing-murdered-indigenous-women-girls/monuments-honouring-mmiwg.
[232] Levack 1999, 8; Hagen 2024, 6.   [233] Dresen-Coenders 1983, 11.
[234] See https://citydays.com/places/the-witches-well/.

(Massachusetts), a city notorious for its witch hysteria in seventeenth-century North America. The monument was designed as the first physical structure in Salem to commemorate the persecution and execution of twenty innocent people – men and mostly women – accused of witchcraft or sorcery in 1692. Inspired by the Vietnam War Memorial, designers Maggie Smith and Jim Cutler wanted the memorial to address the structural gender-specific injustice, by using four themes: silence, deafness, persecution, and memory.[235] Speakers at the unveiling included Holocaust survivor Elie Wiesel who stated: 'In times of inhumanity, humanity is still possible (...). It is because people were fanatic that Salem was possible (...). And fanaticism is the greatest evil that faces us today. For today, too, there are Salems.'[236] In 2017, another memorial in Salem was erected at Proctor's Ledge with input from Salem residents and local historians. It commemorates the executions of Sarah Good, Elizabeth Howe, Susannah Martin, Rebecca Nurse, and Sarah Wildes. Designed by Martha Lyons, the memorial is made up of a circular stone wall featuring engravings of each of the five victim's names.[237]

In the new millennium, more attention has been paid to the history of witch hunts. In several countries, memorials are erected and plaques are placed. For example, the Steilneset Memorial in Vardø in northern Norway, unveiled in 2011, commemorates the burning to death at the stake of 77 women and 14 men.[238] The Belgian city Nieuwpoort rehabilitated seventeen alleged witches (men and women), burned at the stake in the period 1602–1652. They were posthumously cleared of all blame with a commemorative plaque in 2012 (see Figure 24). The mayor stated: 'We are thereby paying off a historical debt by clearing all victims of the witch hunt in our territory of any blame (...). These people fell prey to religious fanaticism, crooked legal proceedings, hatred and gossip and had to pay for it with their lives.'[239] In the Netherlands, the National Witch Memorial Foundation stimulates the creation of a national memorial to the victims of witch burnings, mainly women.[240] The board argues that it is time to raise historical awareness about the witch trials. The National Memorial will be located in the city of Roermond, where in the years 1613–1614 more than 80 so-called female witches were burned alive. The monument, to be realized in 2026, aims to 'contribute to the restoration of the reputations of the victims, raising

---

[235] Shea 2014; see www.theflickeringlamp.org/2014/10/the-salem-witch-trial-memorial-whats.html.
[236] Christiansen and Christ-Doane 2022; see https://folklife.si.edu/magazine/salem-witch-trials-memorial.
[237] See www.hauntedhappenings.org/blog/remembering-salem-witch-trials-memorials/.
[238] www.architecturenorway.no/stories/photo-stories/eggen-steilneset-11/.   [239] Van Loo 2012.
[240] See www.nationaalheksenmonument.nl/.

Figure 24 Memorial plaque with names of alleged witches (1602–1652) as a sign of rehabilitation. Nieuwpoort (Belgium) 2012. Photo Frans90245. https://commons.wikimedia.org/wiki/File:Vliegende_heks_05.jpg

awareness and education around witch persecutions and their cultural heritage in the form of contemporary misogyny, femicide and scapegoating.'[241]

Meanwhile, in recent times, initiatives have been taken in several countries to erect monuments that acknowledge the agency of women, such as female resistance fighters, black civil rights activists, political leaders, inventors and sportswomen. For example, in New York (US) a statue of the famous black abolitionist Harriet Tubman (2021) and in Almere (the Netherlands) a statue for the first black Dutch woman to win an Olympic swimming title Enith Brigitha (2022) are erected.[242] As good and interesting as these initiatives are, if a community wants to achieve mnemonic change and decolonization of public space, more is needed. It means that any decolonizing of a memory landscape should also involve awareness and reflection on the apparent contradiction between human plurality and a public monument.

---

[241] See https://historiek.net/roermond-krijgt-een-nationaal-heksenmonument/169745/.
[242] See www.artsobserver.com/2012/02/19/harriet-tubman-memorial-stands-as-a-symbol-of-fortitude-and-freedom-in-harlem/ and www.omroepflevoland.nl/nieuws/305523/standbeeld-voor-zwemster-enith-brigitha-onthuld.

Monuments as Action and the Implicated Subject

Janet Donohoe's article on Hanna Arendt's theory of the public realm as applied to monuments offers an interesting view about mnemonic change.[243] Arendt, a political philosopher engaged with hermeneutic phenomenology, formulated in 1958 a comprehensive theory of an active life (*vita active*) in contrast to a contemplative life (*vita contemplativa*). Within the *vita activa* Arendt distinguished three fundamental activities that make up the human condition: 'labour', 'work', and 'action'. Labour refers to activities connected to the human body, the household, the provision of biological needs and the maintenance of life, involving general physical care, performed by – what Arendt calls – *animal laborans*.[244] While labour is essential to the survival of the species, work contributes to the construction of the world, such as processing raw materials, using tools, building houses and infrastructures, performed by *homo faber*. According to Arendt: 'The whole factual world of human affairs depends for its reality and its continued existence, first, upon the presence of others who have seen and heard and will remember, and, second, on the transformation of the intangible into the tangibility of things', such as poetry, documents, paintings, sculptures, and monuments.[245] Without the help of *homo faber* – such as artists, poets, historiographers, or 'monument-builders' – the story *homo laborans* enacts and tells would not survive at all.[246]

Action is what Arendt considers the lived experience and political engagement of human activity. It reveals interaction on the one hand and initiative on the other in the public space of appearances: showing oneself in deeds and words, to be seen and heard. Indispensable components of action are: plurality and natality.[247] Human plurality involves the duality of equality and distinction. If human beings were not equal they could not understand each other; if human beings were not distinct they would not interact or make themselves understood.[248] Hence plurality includes the various perspectives of unique but equal human beings. The possibility of articulating different views of the same object or other reality, affirms the commonality of the world. Without it the world would become meaningless and frozen. Natality is the capacity of taking an initiative, starting something new that did not exist before. This sense of initiative is inherent to all human activities. Action as process and outcome are uncontrollable, unpredictable, contingent and creative.[249]

'Work' and 'Action' are relevant for understanding the impact of monuments in public spaces. Monuments as Work affirm dominant ideologies and indicate

---

[243] Donohoe 2016. [244] Arendt 1958, 7; Donohoe 2016, 252. [245] Arendt 1958, 95.
[246] Arendt 1958, 173. [247] Arendt 1958, 8–9. [248] Arendt 1958, 175–176.
[249] Borren and Vasterling 2021, 3.

a desire of people – often leaders – to be remembered forever, to transcend their lives through something that outlives them. Examples are the mimetic state-sanctioned great man statues, which perpetuate narratives as part of a mnemonic regime.[250] However, despite their seemingly eternal materiality, these monuments are always caught up in the passage of time with changing interpretations and emotional effects. They continue the view of a homogeneous and one-dimensional narrative, often about the nation, provoking appreciation and pride or disgust and anger among people who feel offended. The American Confederate statues are an example of this. In themselves these statues refuse plurality; they generally support an ideological and unified meaning that closes off or discourages an opportunity for dialogue.

However, conflicts about monuments can stimulate different views of the past. Due to protests – such as adding critical slogans on pedestals or wrapping statues with a striking cloth – monuments conceived as Work can evolve into Action. Obviously, the difference is not always evident. It is an ideal-type distinction. Both are political speech-acts; but monuments as Action tend to give – in terms of Arendt – more space to natality and plurality. They bring about a sudden interruption of experiencing the world,[251] constituting a surprise and disrupting reality. As creative conceptual innovations, they stimulate dialogues and critical reflection on what is represented, including the processing of – or working through – a traumatized past. The afore-mentioned counter-monuments – the anti-fascist sinking pillar made by the Gerz couple and the mini statues of Kolodko – are monuments as Action par excellence. They mock the very idea of a monument glorifying a person or event for eternity and make visitors aware of older, hegemonic narratives.

Monuments as Action intend to undermine hegemonic narratives and to negate their normative power. As political speech-acts they invite people to reflect critically on past and present, encouraging a plurality of views. They can take visitors and passers-by out of their comfort zone. The aesthetic experience not only attracts attention and arouses wonder, but also demonstrates the power of art. In that sense, public monuments as Action are potential cultural stimuli in the mnemonic change of the memory landscape.[252] Perhaps more importantly, these innovative public monuments can make people also aware of their (indirect) implication in historical processes, regimes, and events, whether colonial exploitation, the transatlantic slave-trade, the Holocaust, Stalinist persecution or organized large-scale sexual violence. In his book *The Implicated Subject* Rothberg argues that each oppressive regime produces a version of 'violent

---

[250] Donohoe 2016, 253–255.   [251] Donohoe 2016, 255–256; Grever 2025A, 387.
[252] Rigney 2021, 14; Grever 2025A.

innocence' of what he calls 'the implicated subject'. Although subjects may not be direct agents of physical violence, they have positions aligned with power and privilege and may still contribute to, benefit from, or be involved in the consequences of such violence across generations, despite spatial and temporal distance.[253] The implicated subject refers to the participant in histories and social formations that generate direct and indirect positions of victim and perpetrator, but in which most people do not occupy such clear-cut roles. With this analytical concept, Rothberg points to the collective, historical legacy of long-term violence – including colonialism and racism – across generations and the associated responsibility.

A striking example encouraging awareness of implication is the temporary public sculpture by Guyanese-British artist Hew Locke, entitled 'Foreign Exchange', unveiled in 2022.[254] Locke both emphasizes and reframes the life-story of Queen Victoria's statue in Birmingham. Rather than remove elements of the figure, the artwork adds layers to it. In a construction of fibre-glass, it fixes Victoria in a crate on a ship, where she is joined on deck by five smaller replicas of herself. The construction shows how the monarch's image was manufactured and shipped across the British Empire, imposing British rule on colonized territories and transmitting British collective memory, resulting in great wealth and power of the empire from which many of its inhabitants benefited.

6 Conclusion

Current conflicts over public monuments can be seen as efforts to change the mnemonic regime of landscapes of memory. This approach reveals five key insights.

First, a monument is rarely a stand-alone phenomenon but is embedded in a landscape of memory with previously erected monuments and statues. Following Ricoeur, these landscapes can therefore be considered as narratives with long-standing canonized stories and marginalized side-stories that (re)shape the human world of actions (Section 2). In this sense, a memory landscape is like a history book with chapters that are connected in a kind of symbolic intertextuality. The mutual relationships of already-there small and large monuments influence public views and interpretations. Walking along memorials and iconic monuments, passers-by attribute different meanings, (re)creating their own narratives. In this way the landscape becomes an actor, generating different (intersubjective) mnemonic experiences. But public monuments are also embedded in a dynamic and global multimedia network, enhancing their

---

[253] Rothberg 2019, 1.   [254] See www.ikon-gallery.org/exhibition/foreign-exchange.

visibility, especially when conflicts about them develop and iconoclastic responses spread into other regions.

Second, memory landscapes can have an alienating effect on people when they feel that their community perspectives are underrepresented or ignored. Protests can then reveal suppressed voices and challenge dominant narratives. Sometimes this results in new monuments, initiated by (formerly) marginalized communities. The actions against Columbus statues across the Americas illustrate this (Section 2). After centuries of oppression and silence, indigenous peoples have finally gained some level of access to public space and can narrate their own culture, reflected in new public monuments. Section 3 also shows the inequality in the commemoration of the dead. For example, it was not until decades later, after the First World War, that monuments were erected to commemorate colonial soldiers and thousands of Chinese workers who came to Europe to dig trenches, remove human remains and bury the dead. Clearly, people need public monuments to mourn and honour the dead, even decades or sometimes centuries later. Ruin encapsulates this need with his concept of necropolitical space, which points to the role of the dead for the maintenance of a political community.

Nevertheless, most governments of former empires have hardly acknowledged their institutional responsibility and – in Rothberg's terms – implicated subject position for the colonial violence committed in the past. Despite the presence of third- and fourth-generation migrants from former colonies – often with ancestors dating back to the slave era – in their countries, most national and city governments seem rather indifferent to these groups' calls for a tangible monument to commemorate their culture. While for them such a public monument in their country of residence offers recognition and restoration of the disrupted necropolitical space, through which the social bond between the living and the dead can be restored. A striking case is the controversy around the Dutch statue of J.P. Coen in Hoorn. Despite the massacre that Coen and his crew committed on Banda in 1621, the statue still stands on the central square four hundred years later. In Section 3, the protests of the Bandanese are interpreted as an attempt to transform the memory landscape in Hoorn and to restore the social bond with the dead. The lack of a public memorial for the murdered ancestors shows – what Stoler calls – colonial aphasia: an occlusion of knowledge, a difficulty in understanding and finding words for the horrors of the colonial past.

Apart from calls to decolonize public space, there is surprisingly little protest that today most memory landscapes are characterized by an overwhelming presence of white men on pedestals (Section 5). In this respect, Fraser's critique on the inherently exclusionary character of public space since the 1790s (Section 2) also applies to memory landscapes, even in the twenty-first century.

Recently, in various countries monuments of (black) female leaders and scientists have been erected. But it would be a mistake to frame public space or a landscape of memory as unchangeably masculine. Public spaces remain sites of contestation with counter-publics that allow for monuments in which the intersectionality of gender, sexuality, race, and class is performed and negotiated.

Three, a major factor in the emergence of controversies about public monuments are size, location, and visual language. It seems that the larger a public statue or monument, the more protest it can provoke. Yet size is not always the decisive factor in conflict. Pent-up anger about ongoing exclusion in memory landscapes can induce damage or destruction. However, this iconoclasm can also express fear of the power of a monument itself. In this sense, protests testify to the hold that public monuments exert over people. At the same time, dismantled statues, empty pedestals, and defaced monuments can shock the public into awareness, breaking a monument's spell. This is especially the case when it concerns carriers of hegemonic memories, such as monuments to Queen Victoria, Confederate statues or the Bronze Soldier in Tallinn (see Section 4). The gaze of passers-by can no longer fix itself on the familiar and the known. The fabric of the memory landscape involved has been disrupted and its implicit ideology exposed. Alternative less destructive responses can also have this effect, exemplified here in the shift during the 1970s and 1980s from mimetic vertical and heroic statues to aniconic and abstract horizontal monuments, acknowledging large-scale wartime violence and genocides. The first, mimetic type usually glorifies the nation or a particular individual and can close off discussion; abstract or aniconic monuments, including those naming the dead (e.g. the Vietnam Veteran Memorial in Washington and the Holocaust Memorial in Berlin) provide room for mourning and grief, stimulating contemplation and dialogue.

The iconography of public monuments is another source of conflict (Section 4). Striking examples are statues of missionaries. Many are depicted with half-naked native young men from the colonies, kneeling at the feet of a fully dressed missionary with a crucifix in his hand. These representations of scantily clad black people evoke strong emotions because they evoke the image of the enslaved 'primitive'. Missionaries are presented as humble icons of mercy with little political power, working for the poor in the colonies, their public statues carrying innocent images of self-sacrifice. In reality they often supported colonialism and endorsed the idea of a civilizing mission, based on a Western conception of progress and white superiority. The white innocence of these statues has been exposed by scholars and activists, as evidenced by several protests against statues of missionaries, such as in the Dutch city of Tilburg.

Four, the controversies surrounding public monuments discussed in this Element show that the combination of tangibility and a specific location is crucial. Stumbling stones placed in front of the house of Holocaust victims are a telling example. Although the stones are small and modest, their exact location and tangibility can trigger or even disturb people (Section 4). An extraordinary case in this respect are the Peace Statues of so-called 'comfort women' (Section 5). The provocative placement of these mimetic life-size statues in front of Japanese embassies in several countries has resulted in debate, political clashes between countries, and international media attention to a previously unspoken history of oppression and violence against women. The statues helped break the taboo surrounding the history of mass rape of women. The conclusion is that despite the embeddedness of public statues and monuments in a dynamic, global media network that facilitates the rapid dissemination of iconoclastic actions across the globe, their tangibility at a specific location in a memory landscape continue to elicit attention, concern, and emotional responses, sometimes resulting in mnemonic change.

Five, changes in memory landscapes often occur through organized public interventions. Sections 4 and 5 show the making of anti-monuments and compensation monuments, initiated by governments, artists, activists, or social movements. This resulted, for example, in the erection of slavery monuments in several European countries and the Freedom Park in Pretoria. These monuments redress the one-sided character of the memory landscape while otherwise leaving intact its fabric and design. Visual artists have also experimented with counter-monuments to disrupt the gaze of passers-by and their interpretations of the past, such as the German anti-fascist monument that slowly sank into the ground. These monuments function, in Hannah Arendt's terms, as Action: as political speech-acts they invite people into a dialogue and encourage critical reflection on past and present, taking them out of their comfort zone.

Conflicts over public monuments keep alive the plurality of the past, but are ultimately also requests to reconfigure the narrative of memory landscapes: not just by adding or replacing statues here and there, but by rethinking its plot. This requires an ongoing process of reflection, creativity and co-creation with descendants, residents, visual artists, and other stakeholders on how to decolonize and diversify existing male-dominated landscapes of memory, keeping the world vital, human, and liveable. No less important, tangible monuments as Action – or dialogical monuments – can make people aware of their responsibility as implicated subjects. They call on passers-by not to look away from oppression and violence in the past, but to examine its depiction in public space and to contemplate their own reactions. In this way, they adduce understanding of the different modes of subject implication and responsibility for human action in past and present.

Bibliography

Alsema, Adriaan, 'Colombia removes statues of Columbus and Spanish Queen after attacks', *Colombia Reports*, 13 June 2021.

Amatmoekrim, Karin, 'Duizenden zwarte soldaten hebben Europa bevrijd, maar hun gezichten zien we amper als we de oorlog herdenken', *De Correspondent*, 16 October 2018.

Ambury, James, 'Towards a Monumental Phenomenology: Paul Ricoeur and the Politics of Memory', *Journal of French and Francophone Philosophy* 16 (2006) 105–120.

Anderson, Benedict, *Imagined Communities: Reflections on the Origins and Spread of Nationalism*. London: Verso, 1983.

Angeleti, Gabriella, 'As monuments to Christopher Columbus come down across the US, Italian-Americans Campaign to Protect a Symbol of "Culture Heritage"', *The Art Newspaper*, 13 August 2020.

Aquino, Catherine L. and Jocelyn S. Martin, 'Twice Removed. The Mystery of Manila's Missing Comfort Woman Monument', in Sarah Gensburger and Jenny Wüstenberg eds., *De-Commemoration: Removing Statues and Renaming Places*. New York/Oxford: Berghahn, 2023, 261–269.

Araujo, Ana L., *Slavery in the Age of Memory: Engaging the Past*. London: Bloomsbury, 2021.

Arendt, Hannah, *The Human Condition*. Chicago: The University of Chicago Press, 1958 (repr. 2018).

Assmann, Jan, 'Communicative and Cultural Memory', in Astrid Erll and Ansgar Nünning eds., *Cultural Memory Studies: An International and Interdisciplinary Handbook*. Berlin: De Gruyter, 2008, 109–118.

Assmann, Aleida, *Der lange Schatten der Vergangenheit: Erinnerungskultur und Geschichtspolitik*. München: C.H. Beck Verlag, 2006.

Bailey, Paul, 'From "Coolie" to Transnational Agent. The "Afterlives" of World War One Chinese Workers', in Ben Wellings and Shanti Sumartojo eds., *Commemorating Race and Empire in the First World War Centenary*. Liverpool: Liverpool University Press, 2018, 23–38.

Balkenhol, Markus, 'Colonial Heritage and the Sacred: Contesting the Statue of Jan Pieterszoon Coen in the Netherlands', in Markus Balkenhol, Ernst van den Hemel and Irene Stengs eds., *The Secular Sacred: Emotions of Belonging and the Perils of Nation and Religion*. Basingstoke: Palgrave Macmillan, 2020, 195–216.

Banning, Jan, *Comfort Women: Troostmeisjes*. Berlin: Seltmann Publishers GmbH, 2012.

Binter, Julia ed., *The Blind Spot. Bremen, Colonialism and Art*. Bremen: Kunsthalle, 2017.

Blaas, Piet B. M. (Piet), *Geschiedenis en nostalgie: De historiografie van een kleine natie met een groot verleden*. Hilversum: Verloren, 2000.

Borren, Marieke and Veronica Vasterling, 'Hannah Arendt'. *Bloomsbury History: Theory & Method* (2021). Online resource. Section Key-thinkers (15 p.). DOI: 10.5040/9781350927933.123. See https://www.bloomsburyhis torytheorymethod.com/article?docid=b-9781350927933&tocid=b-9781350927933-123&st=Hannah+Arendt.

Branscome, Eva, 'Colston's Travels, or Should We Talk About Statues?', *Arena Journal of Architectural Research* 6 (2021) 1–29.

Brito, Christopher, 'Dozens of Christopher Columbus Statues Have Been Removed Since June', *CBS News* 25 September 2020 (www.cbsnews.com/news/christopher-columbus-statue-removed-cities/).

Çelik, Zeynep, 'Colonial Statues and their Afterlives', *The Journal of North African Studies* 25 (2020) 711–726.

Chapman, David, 'Visualising Korea: The Politics of the Statue of Peace', *Asian Studies Review* 45 (2021) 420–434.

Christiansen, Jill and Rachel Christ-Doane, 'The Salem Witch Trials Memorial: Finding Humanity in Tragedy', *Folk Life Magazine*, 22 October 2022.

Code, Chris and Brian Petheram, 'Delivering for Aphasia', *International Journal of Speech-Language Pathology* 13 (2011) 3–10.

Colard, Sandrine, 'Introduction to the Report "Decolonizing Public Spaces in the Brussels-Capital Region"', *Appropriations* 2023 (www.e-flux.com/archi tecture/appropriations/533413/introduction-to-the-report-decolonizing-pub lic-spaces-in-the-brussels-capital-region/).

Colenbrander, Herman T., *Jan Pietersz. Coen. Bescheiden omtrent zijn bedrijf in Indië*. Den Haag: M. Nijhoff, 1919.

Cook, Matthew and Micheline van Riemsdijk, 'Agents of Memorialization: Gunther Demnig's Stolpersteine and the Individual (Re-)creation of a Holocaust Landscape in Berlin', *Journal of Historical Geography* 43 (2014) 138–147.

Dankelman, Jan L., *Peerke Donders: Schering en inslag van zijn leven*. Hilversum: Gooi en Sticht, 1982.

De Baets, Antoon, 'The Posthumous Dignity of Dead Persons', in Roberto C. Parra and Douglas H. Ubelaker eds., *Anthropology of Violent Death: Theoretical Foundations for Forensic Humanitarian Action*. Hoboken: John Wiley & Sons, 2023, 15–37.

De Vries, Lucia, *Vrouwen op sokkels: De achterstelling van vrouwen binnen de Nederlandse standbeeldencultuur*. Master Thesis. Nijmegen: Radboud Universiteit, 2021.

Demetriou, Dan and Ajume Wingo, 'The Ethics of Racist Monuments', *Philosophy Publications* 6 (2018) 1–19.

Díaz Tovar, Alfonso, 'Antimonumentos. Espacio público, memoria y duelo social en México', *Aletheia* 8 (2018) 16.

Dickenson, Christopher P. ed., *Public Statues across Times and Cultures*. London: Routledge, 2021.

Donoe, Janet, 'Hannah Arendt and the Ideological Character of Monuments', in Stuart West Gurley and Geoff Pfeifer eds., *Phenomenology and the Political*. Washington, DC: Rowman & Littlefield Publishers, 2016, 251–262.

Dresen-Coenders, Lène, *Het Verbond van heks en duivel: een waandenkbeeld aan het begin van de moderne tijd als symptoom van een veranderende situatie van de vrouw en als middel tot hervorming der zeden*. Amsterdam: AMBO, 1983.

Driessen, Henk, *Terug naar de Spaanse Burgeroorlog: etnografie en het onvoltooid verleden*. Amsterdam: AUP, 2013.

Erll, Astrid and Ann Rigney, eds. *Mediation, Remediation and the Dynamics of Cultural Memory*. Berlin/New York: De Gruyter, 2009.

Erll, Astrid, 'Travelling Memory', *Parallax* 7 (2011) 4–18.

Eröss, Ágnes, 'Landscape in Transition in the Shadow of 2022 Russia's Invasion in Ukraine – Notes from Hungary', *Border and Regional Studies* 10 (2022) 71–86.

Eskes, Mathijs, 'De slagen om Ieper als herinneringslandschap. Land van modder, staal en vlees', *Historiek*, 26 May 2023.

Essed, Philomena and Isabel Hoving, 'Innocence, Smug Ignorance, Resentment: an Introduction to Dutch Racism', in Philomena Essed and Isabel Hoving eds., *Dutch Racism*. Amsterdam: Rhodopi, 2014, 9–29.

Fazio, Marie, 'Boston Removes Statue of Formerly Enslaved Man Kneeling Before Lincoln', *New York Times*, 29 December 2020.

Ferrell, Robert, *Unjustly Dishonored: An African American Division in World War I*. Columbia and London: University of Missouri Press, 2011.

Fitters, Herman, 'Peerke en het verdeelde verleden. Helend verwerken: mission impossible of Heilige opgave?', *Working Group Caribbean Literature*, 06 June 2020.

Fraser, Nancy, 'Rethinking the Public Sphere: A Contribution to the Critique of Actually Existing Democracy', *Social Text* 25 (1990) 26, 56–80.

Frederickson, George M., *Racism: A Short History*. Princeton: Princeton University Press, 2002.

Freedberg, David, 'The Fear of Art: How Censorship Becomes Iconoclasm', *Social Research* 83 (2016) Spring, 67–99.

Frei, Cheryl J., 'Columbus, Juana and the Politics of Plaza: Battles over Monuments, Memory and Identity in Buenos Aires', *Journal of Latin American Studies* 51 (2019) 607–638.

Gatugu, Clara, 'The Decolonization of Belgian Public Space', *Justice & Paix*, 28 October 2022.

Gensburger, Sarah and Jenny Wüstenberg, 'Introduction. Making Sense of De-Commemoration', in Sarah Gensburger and Jenny Wüstenberg eds., *De-Commemoration: Removing Statues and Renaming Places*. New York/Oxford: Berghahn, 2023, 1–15.

Ghosh, Amitav, *The Nutmeg's Curse: Parables for a Planet in Crisis*. London: John Murray, 2021.

Gill, Michael, *Image of the Body: Aspects of the Nude*. London/New York: Doubleday, 1989.

Goddeeris, Idesbald, *Missionarissen: Geschiedenis, Herinnering, Dekolonisering*. Leuven: Lannoo Campus, 2021.

Goddeeris, Idesbald, 'Belgian Monuments of Colonial Violence: The Commemoration of Martyred Missionaries', *Journal of Genocide Research* 4 (2022) 586–603.

Grever, Maria, 'Colonial Queens: Imperialism, Gender and the Body Politic during the Reign of Victoria and Wilhelmina', *Dutch Crossing: A Journal of Low Countries* 26 (2002) 99–114.

Grever, Maria, 'Teaching the War: Reflections on Popular Uses of Difficult Heritage', in Terrie Epstein and Carla L. Peck eds., *Teaching and Learning Difficult Histories in International Contexts. A Critical Sociocultural Approach*. New York: Routledge, 2018, 30–44.

Grever, Maria, 'Historical Consciousness and Contested Statues in a Post-Colonial World: The Case of Missionary Peerke Donders', *History of Education* 52 (2023) 1000–1014.

Grever, Maria, 'Verhalen op sokkels. Omstreden monumenten in een veranderend herinneringslandschap', *Holland Historisch Tijdschrift* 56 (2024) no. 4, 148–158.

Grever, Maria, 'Monuments as Actants of Mnemonic Change', in Astrid Erll, Susanne Knittel and Jenny Wüstenberg eds., *Dynamics Mediation Mobilisation: Doing Memory Studies With Ann Rigney*. Berlin: De Gruyter, 2025A, 383–388.

Grever, Maria, 'Traces of Existence. Public Monuments and the Dead', *Rethinking History: The Journal of Theory and Practice* 29 (2025B) no. 2, 336–356 .

Grever, Maria and Berteke Waaldijk, *Transforming the Public Sphere: The Dutch National Exhibition of Women's Labor in 1898*. Durham: Duke University Press, 2004.

Grever, Maria and Susan Legêne, 'Histories of an Old Empire. The Ever-Changing Acknowledgement of Dutch Imperialism as a Present Past', in Ander Delgado and Andrew Mycock eds., *Conflicts in History Education in Europe: Political Context, History Teaching and National Identity*. Charlotte NC: IAP-Information Age, 2024, 27–47.

Gropas, Maria, 'The Repatriotization of Revolutionary Ideology and Mnemonic Landscape in Present-Day Havana', *Current Anthropology* 48 (2007) 531–549.

Gqola, Pumla Dineo, Iromi Perera, Shilpa Phadke, et al., 'Gender and Public Space', *Gender & Development* 23 (2024) 1–25.

Gutiérrez, Fernando, 'Spaces for Resistance, Places for Remembering: The Anti-Monumenta in Mexico City', *Urban Matters*, 31 October 2024.

Habermas, Jürgen, *The Structural Transformation of the Public Sphere: An Inquiry into a Category of Bourgeois Society*. Cambridge, MA: MIT Press, 1989.

Hagen, Rune Blix, 'The Era of Early Modern Witch Hunts in Europe', *Midgard Talks*, 14 August 2024.

Harris, Cheryl, 'Whiteness as Property', *Harvard Law Review* 106 (1993) 1707–1791.

Hatt, Michael, 'Counter Ceremonial: Contemporary Artists and Queen Victoria Monuments', *Interdisciplinary Studies in the Long Nineteenth Century* 33 (2022) 1–28.

Heuser, Dillon, *Onderzoeksrapport slavernijverleden van Hoorn*. Rotterdam: Stad & Bedrijf, 2023.

Hondius, Dienke, Nancy Jouwe, Dineke Stam and Jennifer Tosch, *Gids Slavernijverleden Nederland: Slavery Heritage Guide the Netherlands*. Volendam: LM Publishers, 2019.

Huyssen, Andreas, 'Monument and Memory in a Postmodern Age', in James Young ed., *Holocaust Memorials. The Art of Memory in History*. New York: Prestel Verlag, 1994, 9–17.

Janssen, Hilde, *Schaamte en onschuld: Het verdrongen verleden van troostmeisjes in Indonesië*. Amsterdam: Boom, 2010.

Jawanda, Jasmindra, 'Decolonizing and Reimagining Urban Public Spaces with Art from Indigenous/Black/People of Colour Communities', *Primary Colours/Couleurs primaires* (2022) (www.primary-colours.ca/projects/154-decolonizing-and-reimagining-urban-public-spaces-with-art-from-indigenous-black-people-of-colour-communities).

Johnson, Nuala C., 'Locating Memory: Tracing the Trajectories of Remembrance', *Historical Geography* 33 (2005) 165–179.

Kapp, Paul Hardin, 'Conservation, Tradition and Popular Iconoclasm in North America', *The Historic Environment: Policy and Practice* 11 (2021) 97–115.

Kerby, Martin C., Margaret Baguley, Richard Gehrmann and Alison Bedford, *A Possession Forever: A Guide to Using Commemorative Memorials and Monuments in the Classroom*. Toowoomba: University of Queensland, 2021.

Kim, Joohee, 'Going Transnational? A Feminist View of "Comfort Women" Memorials', *Asian Journal of Women Studies* 26 (2022) 3, 397–409.

KNAW, *Wankele sokkels: Omstreden monumenten in de openbare ruimte* (*Unstable Pedestals. Contested Monuments in Public Spaces*). Amsterdam: KNAW, 2023.

Kolen, Jan, Johannes Renes and Rita Hermans eds., *Landscape Biographies. Geographical, Historical and Archaeological Perspectives on the Production and Transmission of Landscapes*. Amsterdam: Amsterdam University Press, 2015.

Koselleck, Reinhart. 'Einleitung', in Koselleck, Reinhart und Michael Jeismann Hrsg., *Der politische Totenkult. Kriegerdenkmäler in der Moderne*. München: Fink, 1994, 9–20.

Koselleck, Reinhart., *Geronnene Lava: Texte zu politischem Totenkult und Erinnerung*. Berlin: Suhrkamp Verlag, 2023 (posthumously published compilation of Koselleck's essays).

Kopytoff, Igor, 'The Cultural Biography of Things: Commoditization as Process', in Arjun Appadurai ed., *The Social Life of Things: Commodities in Cultural Perspective*. Cambridge: Cambridge University Press, 1986, 64–91.

Kouzelis, Athanasios, Magnus Rönn and Helena Teräväinen eds., *Compensation in Architecture and Archaeology. On Compensation as a Project, Method and Professional Practice*. Gotenburg: Kulturlandskapet & Chalmers University of Technology, 2022.

Kruyswijk, Marc, 'Bewoners Oud-Zuid naar rechter om struikelsteen', *Het Parool*, 31 March 2017.

Labuschagne, Pieter, 'Monument(al) Meaning Making of the "New" South Africa: Freedom Park as a Symbol of a New Identity and Freedom?', *South African of Art History* 25 (2010) 112–124.

Laqueur, Thomas, *The Work of the Dead: A Cultural History of Mortal Remains*. Princeton: Princeton University Press, 2015.

Latour, Bruno, *Reassembling the Social: An Introduction to Actor-Network-Theory*. Oxford: Oxford University Press, 2005.

Larsen, Laragh, 'Re-placing Imperial Landscapes: Colonial Monuments and the Transition to Independence in Kenya', *Journal of Historical Geography* 38 (2012) 45–56.

Levack, Brian P., 'The Decline and End of Witchcraft Prosecutions', in Marijke Gijswijt-Hofstra, Brian Levack and Roy Porter, *Witchcraft and Magic in Europe: The Eighteenth and Nineteenth Centuries vol. 5*. London: The Athlone Press, 1999, 1–91.

Levine, Philippa, 'States of Undress: Nakedness and the Colonial Imagination', *Victoria Studies* 50 (2008) 189–219.

Levy, Daniel and Natan Sznaider, *Human Rights and Memory*. Pennsylvania: Penn State University Press, 2010.

Lindsay, Suzanne G., 'The Revolutionary Exhumations at St-Denis, 1793', *Conversations: An Online Journal of the Center for the Study of Material and Visual Cultures of Religion* (2015) (https://doi.org/10.22332/con.ess.2015.2; https://mavcor.yale.edu/conversations/essays/revolutionary-exhumations-st-denis-1793).

Lindström, Kati, 'Landscape Image as a Mnemonic Tool in Cultural Change: The Case of Two Phantom Sceneries', *Place and Location: Studies in Environmental Aesthetics and Semiotics* VI (2008) 227–238.

Ling, Cheah Wu, 'Walking the Long Road in Solidarity and Hope: A Case Study of the "Comfort Women" Movement's Deployment of Human Rights Discourse', *Harvard Human Rights Journal* 22 (2009) 63–107.

Loth, Vincent, 'Pioneers and Perkeniers: the Banda Islands in the 18th Century', *Cakalele* 6 (1995) 13–35.

Mak, Geertje, Marit Monteiro and Elisabeth Wessseling, 'Child Separation. (Post)Colonial Policies and Practices in the Netherlands and Belgium', *BMGN – Low Countries Historical Review* 135 (2020) 4–28.

Malpas, Jeff ed., *The Place of Landscape: Concepts, Contexts, Studies*. Cambridge/London: MIT Press, 2011.

Manuhutu, Wim, Glenda Pattipeilohy and Henry Timisela eds., *70 Jaar Molukkers*, Zutphen: Walburg Pers, 2021.

Matteo, Virginia, 'Remembering Franco's Legacy: How Spain Broke the Pact of Forgetting', *Owlcation* (2023) (https://owlcation.com/humanities/Pact-of-Forgetting-el-Pacto-del-Olvido-Francos-Spain).

Maus, Gunnar, 'Landscapes of Memory: A Practice Theory Approach to Geographies of Memory', *Geographica Helvetica* 70 (2015) 215–223.

McCarthy, Mary, 'US Comfort Women Memorials: Vehicles for Understanding and Change', *Asia Pacific Bulletin* no. 275, 12 August 2014, 1–2.

Modest, Wayne, 'Voorwoord. Van stilte naar "mapping": (re)presentaties van slavernij'/'Forword. From Silence to "Mapping": (Re)Presenting Slavery

Histories', in Dienke Hondius, Nancy Jouwe, Dineke Stam, and Jennifer Tosch, eds., *Gids Slavernijverleden Nederland: Slavery Heritage Guide the Netherlands*. Volendam: LM Publishers, 2019, VI–IX.

Monteiro, Marit, 'Colonial Complicities: Catholic Missionaries, Chinese Elite and Non-Kin Support for Chinese Children in Semarang during the 1930s', *BMGN – Low Countries Historical Review* 135 (2020) 158–183.

Moreton-Robinson, Aileen, *The White Possessive: Property, Power, and Indigenous Sovereignty*. Minneapolis: University of Minnesota Press, 2015

Mosse, George, *Fallen Soldiers: Reshaping the Memory of the World Wars*. New York/Oxford: Oxford University Press, 1990.

Nederveen Pieterse, Jan, *Wit over zwart: Beelden van Afrika en zwarten in de westerse populaire cultuur*. Amsterdam: NOVIB, 1990, 52–62.

Ngugi, Thiong'o wa, *Decolonising the Mind: The Politics of Language in African Literature*. London and Portmouth: Pearson Education, 1986.

Oestigaard, Terje and Joakim Goldhahn, 'From the Dead to the Living: Death as Transactions and Re-negotiations', *Norwegian Archaeological Review* 39 (2006) 1, 27–48.

Olko, Justyna, 'Body Language in the Preconquest and Colonial Nahua World', *Ethnohistory* 61 (2014) Winter, 149–179.

Oostindie, Gert, *Postcolonial Netherlands: Sixty-Five Years of Forgetting, Commemorating, Silencing*. Amsterdam: Amsterdam University Press, 2011.

Otele, Olivette, 'Bristol, Slavery and the Politics of Representation: The Slave Trade Gallery in the Bristol Museum', *Social Semiotics* 22 (2012) 155–172.

Perreault, Tom, 'Mining, Meaning and Memory in the Andes', *The Geographical Journal* 184 (2018) 229–241.

Petrig, Anna (2009). 'The War Dead and their Gravesites', *International Review of the Red Cross* 91 (2009) 342–369.

Plokhy, Serhii, *The Russo-Ukrainian War: The Return of History*. New York: Norton, 2023.

Plümer-Bardak, Esra ed., *A Space of our Own: A Handbook on Gender and Monuments in intersectional Public Spaces*. Nicosia: The Association for Historical Dialogue and Research, 2023.

Plunkett, John, 'A Tale of Two Statues: Memorializing Queen Victoria in London and Calcutta', *19 Interdisciplinary Studies in the Long Nineteenth Century* 33 (2022) 1–32.

Prescott, Cynthia C. and Janne Lahti, 'Looking Globally at Monuments, Violence and Colonial Legacies', *Journal of Genocide Research* 24 (2022) 463–470.

Ramirez, Andres, 'Decolonizing the National Park: Unsettling Public Space through Indigenous Urbanism', *Journal of Race, Ethnicity and the City* 6 (2024), no. 1, 38–65.

Rassool, Ciraj, 'Re-storing the Skeletons of Empire: Return, Reburial and Rehumanisation in Southern Africa', *Journal of Southern African Studies* 41 (2015) 3, 653–670.

Réau, Louis, *Histoire du vandalisme: Les monuments détruits de l'Art français*. Paris: Hachette, 1959.

Reston, James Jr., 'The Monument Glut', *New York Times*, 10 September 1995.

Ricoeur, Paul, *Time and Narrative* I-III. Chicago: The University of Chicago Press, 1984 and 1988.

Ricoeur, Paul, 'Life in Quest of Narrative', in David Wood ed., *On Paul Ricoeur: Narrative and Interpretation*. New York: Routledge, 1991, 20–33.

Ricoeur, Paul, *Memory, History, Forgetting*. Chicago/London: The University of Chicago Press, 2004.

Ricoeur, Paul, 'Architecture and Narrativity', *Ricoeur Studies* 7 (2016) 31–41.

Rigney, Ann, 'Remembering Hope: Transnational Activism Beyond the Traumatic', *Memory Studies* 11 (2018) 368–380.

Rigney, Ann, 'Remaking Memory and the Agency of the Aesthetic', *Memory Studies* 14 (2021)1, 10–23.

Rigney, Ann, 'Toxic Monuments and Mnemonic Regime Change', *Studies on National Movements* 9 (2022) 7–40.

Rigney, Ann, 'Decommissioning Monuments, Mobilizing Materialities', in Yifat Gutman and Jenny Wüstenberg eds., *Routledge Handbook of Memory Activism*. London/New York: Routledge, 2023, 21–27.

Robben, Petra, 'Katholiek of koloniaal? De veranderende waardering van het standbeeld van Peerke Donders', *Tilburg. Tijdschrift voor geschiedenis, monumenten en cultuur* 38 (2020) no. 1, 3–12.

Rofe, Matthew and Michael Ripmeester, 'Memorial Landscapes and Contestation: Destabilising Artefacts of Stability', *Landscape Research* 48 (2023) 609–614.

Ross, Marc Howard, *Cultural Contestation in Ethnic Conflict*. Cambridge: Cambridge University Press, 2007.

Rothberg, Michael, *The Implicated Subject: Beyond Victims and Perpetrators*. Stanford: Stanford University Press, 2019.

Ruin, Hans, *Being with the Dead: Burial, Ancestral Politics, and the Roots of Historical Consciousness*. Stanford: Stanford University Press, 2018.

Ryback, Timothy W., Mark S. Ellis and Benjamin Glahn eds., *Contested Histories in Public Spaces. Principles, Processes, Best Practices*. London: International Bar Association, 2021 (https://contestedhistories.org/onsite/).

Said, Edward, *Culture and Imperialism*. London: Vintage, 1994.

Samuels, Marwyn, 'The Biography of Landscape. Cause and Culpability', in Donald Meinig ed., *The Interpretation of Ordinary Landscapes: Geographical Essays*. New York/Oxford: Oxford University Press, 1979, 51–88.

Savage, Kirk, *Monument Wars: Washington, DC, the National Mall, and the Transformation of the Memorial Landscape*. Berkeley: University of California Press, 2009.

Scates, Bruce and Peter Yu, 'De-Colonizing Australia's Commemorative Landscape: "Truth-Telling", Contestation and the Dialogical Turn', *Journal of Genocide Research* 24 (2022) 488–510.

Schama, Simon, *Landscape and Memory*. New York: Alfred A. Knopf: 1995.

Schönfeldt-Aultman, Scott M., 'Monument(al) Meaning-Making: The Ncome Monument and its Representation of Zulu identity', *Journal of African Cultural Studies* 18 (2006) 215–234.

Seligmann-Silva, Márcio, 'Antimonuments: Between Memory and Resistance', *Between* X 20 (2020) 148–169.

Shane, Leo, 'Protesters Damage Veterans Affairs Headquarters, Several DC War Monuments', *Military Times*, 01 June 2020.

Shanken, Andrew M., *The Everyday Life of Memorials*. Princeton: Princeton University Press, 2022.

Sheldrake, Philip, 'Garden, City, or Wilderness? Landscape and Destiny in the Christian Imagination', in Malpas ed., *The Place of Landscape*, 2011, 183–201.

Shim, David, 'Memorials' Politics: Exploring the Material Rhetoric of the Statue of Peace', *Memory Studies* 16 (2023) 663–676.

Simko, Christina, David Cunningham and Nicole Fox, 'Contesting Commemorative Landscapes: Confederate Monuments and Trajectories of Change', *Social Problems* 69 (2022) 3, 591–611.

Solano, Lorena A., 'Puerto Resistancia: Anti-Monuments, Memory and Mourning', *Urban Matters*, 30 October 2024.

Solnit, Rebecca, 'The Monument Wars', *Harper's Magazine*, EASY CHAIR, 10–13 January 2017.

Steijlen, Fridus, 'Willy Nanlohy vs J.P. Coen', *MHM Nieuwsbrief*, 16 June 2015 (https://museum-maluku.nl/willy-nanlohy-vs-jp-coen/).

Steijlen, Fridus, *Tjakalele at Full Moon* (Inaugural Address). Amsterdam: Vrije Universiteit Amsterdam, 2018.

Stoler, Ann Laura, 'Colonial Aphasia: Race and Disabled Histories in France', *Public Culture* 23 (2011) 121–156.

Tacke, Charlotte, *Denkmal im sozialen Raum: Nationale Symbole in Deutschland und Frankreich im 19. Jahrhundert.* Göttingen: Vandenhoeck & Ruprecht, 1995.

Tamm, Marek, 'In Search of Lost Time. Memory Politics in Estonia, 1991-2011', *Nationalities Papers* 41 (2013) 651–674.

Tongsuthi, Janet, '"Comfort Women" of World War II', *UCLA Women's Law Journal* 4 (1994) 413–419.

Üngör, Ugur Ümit, 'Cultural Genocide: Destruction of Material and Non-Material Human Culture', in Cathie Carmichael and Richard C. Maguire eds., *The Routledge History of Genocide*. London: Routledge, 2015, 241–254.

Ushiyama, Rin, '"Comfort Women Must Fall?" Japanese Governmental Responses to "Comfort Women" Statues Around the World', *Memory Studies* 14 (2021) 6.

Van der Schriek, Max, 'Landscape Biographies of Commemoration', *Landscape Research* 44 (2019) 99–111.

Van der Vlies, Tina, 'History Textbooks as Discursive Mediators: The Case of Dutch Tolerance, 1920-1990', in Henrik Edgren, Merethe Roos and Johannes Westberg eds., *Secular Schooling in the Long Twentieth Century? Christianity and Education in Norway, Sweden, and the Netherlands.* Oldenbourg: De Gruyter, 2024, 223–243.

Van Donkersgoed, Joëlla, 'Shifting the Historical Narrative of the Banda Islands: From Colonial Violence to Local Resilience', *Wacana. Journal of the Humanities of Indonesia* 24 (2023), no. 3, 500–514.

Van Dijk, Marit, *The Hegemonic Influence of the Post-Imperial Landscape on Collective Memory: Walking and Talking in Amsterdam*. Cork: University College Cork, 2017.

Van Engelenhoven, Gerlov, *Postcolonial Memory in the Netherlands: Meaningful Voices, Meaningful Silences*. Amsterdam: Amsterdam University Press, 2022.

Van Goor, Jur, *Jan Pieterszoon Coen 1587–1629: Koopman-koning in Azië*. Amsterdam: Boom, 2015.

Van Houwelingen, Hans, 'The Monument of Shame: Why Dishonor Must Become Part of Commemorative Practices', *Arts of the Working Class*, December 3, 2020 (https://artsoftheworkingclass.org/text/on-the-monument-of-shame).

Van Loo, Dany, 'Heksen en ketters krijgen eerherstel op 30 juni', *Nieuwsblad*, 20 June 2012 (www.nieuwsblad.be/regio/west-vlaanderen/heksen-en-ketters-krijgen-eerherstel-op-30-juni/58693612.html).

Van Ruyskensvelde, Sarah and Mieke Berghmans, 'Toward a Decolonial Praxis in History of Education Research: An Exploration of the Conversations as a Collective Study Practice', *Encounters in Theory and History of Education* 25 (2024) 127–151.

Van Stipriaan, Alex, 'Disrupting the Canon: the Case of Slavery', in Maria Grever and Siep Stuurman eds., *Beyond the Canon: History in the Twenty-First Century*. Basingstoke: Palgrave Macmillan, 2007, 205–219.

Villamil-Valencia, Mateo, 'Existing Everywhere: Urban Layers of Memories and Mourning Landscapes in the Global South', *Urban Matters*, 4 November 2024.

Vosloo, Piet and Graham Young, 'Isivivane, Freedom Park: a Critical Analysis of the Relationship between Commemoration, Meaning and Landscape Design in Post-Apartheid South Africa', *Acta Structilia* 27 (2020) 85–118.

Wagoner, Brady and Ignacio Brescó, 'Memorials as Healing Places: A Matrix for Bridging Material Design and Visitor Experience', *International Journal of Environmental Research and Public Health* 19 (2022) 1–19.

Ward, Thomas, 'The Comfort Women Controversy – Lessons from Taiwan', *The Asia Pacific Journal* 16 (2018) issue 8, no. 5.

Watkins, Nicolas, Frances Cole and Sue Weidemann, 'The War Memorial as Healing Environment: the Psychological Effect of the Vietnam Veterans Memorial on Vietnam Combat Veterans' Posttraumatic Stress Disorder Symptoms', *Environment and Behavior* 42 (2010) 351–375.

Waxman, Olivia, 'How Christopher Columbus Became an Italian-American Icon', *Time*, 8 October 2021.

Weisser, Christian R., 'Subaltern Counterpublics and the Discourse of Protest', *JAC* 28 (2008) 608–620.

Wekker, Gloria, *White Innocence: Paradoxes of Colonialism and Race*. Durham: Duke University Press, 2016.

Wildeboer Schut, Rachelle and Zoltán Dujisin, 'Spain's Democratic Anxieties Through the Lens of Franco's Reburial', *Memory Studies* 16 (2022) 4, 837–860.

Winston, Janet, 'Queen Victoria in the Funnyhouse: Adrienne Kennedy and the Rituals of Colonial Possession', in Margaret Homans and Adrienne Munch eds., *Remaking Queen Victoria*. Cambridge: Cambridge University Press, 1997, 235–257.

Wolfson, Elisabeth, 'The "Black Gash of Shame" – Revisiting the Vietnam Veterans Memorial Controversy', *art21 Magazine*, March/April 2017.

Woods Masalski, Kathleen, 'Examining the Japanese History Textbook Controversies', *Japan Digest*, November 2001.

Xu, Guoqi, *Strangers on the Western Front: Chinese Workers in the Great War*. Cambridge, MA: Harvard University Press, 2011.

Young, James, 'The Counter-Monument: Memory against Itself in Germany Today', *Critical Inquiry* 18 (Winter 1992) 267–296.

Young, Robert J. C., *Colonial Desire: Hybridity in Theory, Culture and Race*. New York: Routledge, 1995.

Acknowledgements

This Element emerged from my work as chair of the Contested Monuments Committee for the Royal Netherlands Academy of Arts and Sciences (KNAW). The advice report, focusing on Dutch monuments and statues, was published in October 2023. I thank the committee for their expert input and inspiring conversations: Paul van Geest, Hans van Houwelingen, Gert Oostindie, Ann Rigney, Jennifer Tosh, Harry Tupan, and Uğur Ümit Üngör.

In this Element the scope has been considerably expanded. Conflicts over public monuments are approached as an attempt to change the mnemonic regime in landscapes of memory, illustrated by trans-national and global cases. Second, specific theoretical concepts will provide further insights into the meaning and background of public monumental conflicts and the effects on mnemonic change.

I am very grateful to Daniel Woolf for his support and his always prompt responses. Also many thanks to Tina van der Vlies for carefully reading the entire manuscript and giving valuable comments, and to Robbert-Jan Adriaansen for his useful feedback on a draft section. Finally, I would like to thank the anonymous reviewers.

Cambridge Elements

Historical Theory and Practice

Daniel Woolf
Queen's University, Ontario

Daniel Woolf is Professor of History at Queen's University, where he served for ten years as Principal and Vice-Chancellor, and has held academic appointments at a number of Canadian universities. He is the author or editor of several books and articles on the history of historical thought and writing, and on early modern British intellectual history, including most recently *A Concise History of History* (CUP 2019). He is a Fellow of the Royal Historical Society, the Royal Society of Canada, and the Society of Antiquaries of London. He is married with three adult children.

Editorial Board
Dipesh Chakrabarty, *University of Chicago*
Marnie Hughes-Warrington, *University of South Australia*
Ludmilla Jordanova, *University of Durham*
Angela McCarthy, *University of Otago*
María Inés Mudrovcic, *Universidad Nacional de Comahue*
Herman Paul, *Leiden University*
Stefan Tanaka, *University of California, San Diego*
Richard Ashby Wilson, *University of Connecticut*

About the Series
Cambridge Elements in Historical Theory and Practice is a series intended for a wide range of students, scholars, and others whose interests involve engagement with the past. Topics include the theoretical, ethical, and philosophical issues involved in doing history, the interconnections between history and other disciplines and questions of method, and the application of historical knowledge to contemporary global and social issues such as climate change, reconciliation and justice, heritage, and identity politics.

Cambridge Elements

Historical Theory and Practice

Elements in the Series

Conceptualizing the History of the Present Time
María Inés Mudrovcic

Writing the History of the African Diaspora
Toyin Falola

Dealing with Dark Pasts: A European History of Auto-Critical Memory in Global Perspective
Itay Lotem

A Human Rights View of the Past
Antoon De Baets

Historians' Autobiographies as Historiographical Inquiry: A Global Perspective
Jaume Aurell

Historiographic Reasoning
Aviezer Tucker

Pragmatism and Historical Representation
Serge Grigoriev

History And Hermeneutics
Paul Fairfield

Testimony and Historical Knowledge: Authority, Evidence and Ethics in Historiography
Jonas Ahlskog

Things of the Past: A Modern Yearning
Kasper Risbjerg Eskildsen

Race, Genetics, History: New Practices, New Approaches
Alexandra P. Alberda, Njabulo Chipangura, Lara Choksey, Jerome de Groot and Maya Sharma

Contested Public Monuments: Global Perspectives on Landscapes of Memory
Maria Grever

A full series listing is available at: www.cambridge.org/EHTP

For EU product safety concerns, contact us at Calle de José Abascal, 56–1°,
28003 Madrid, Spain or eugpsr@cambridge.org.

www.ingramcontent.com/pod-product-compliance
Lightning Source LLC
LaVergne TN
LVHW011849060526
838200LV00054B/4250